W9-BSR-852

Let's Talk About
the Metric System

LET'S TALK ABOUT
THE METRIC SYSTEM

BY JOYCE LAMM

JONATHAN DAVID PUBLISHERS, INC.
MIDDLE VILLAGE, N.Y. 11379

LET'S TALK ABOUT THE METRIC SYSTEM
Copyright © 1974
by
Joyce Lamm
No part of this book may be reproduced in any manner
without written permission from the publishers.
Address all inquiries to:

JONATHAN DAVID PUBLISHERS
Middle Village, New York 11379

Printed in the United States of America

Library of Congress Cataloging in Publication Data

Lamm, Joyce.
Let's talk about the metric system.

SUMMARY: An introduction to the history,
principles, and uses of the metric system including
sample problems, charts, and conversion tables.
1. Metric system—Juvenile literature.
[1. Metric system] I. Title.
QC92.5.L35   389'.152   73-80415
ISBN 0-8246-0158-0

EXTENSION

76 30528

Table of Contents

PHOTO CREDITS

U.S. National Bureau of Standards; Bureau International des Poids et Mesures; U.S. Metric Information Office; Ford Motor Company; John Deere Company; NASA; Association of American Railroads; Swiss National Tourist Office; Inf. Can. Phototheque (Canadian Government Photo Center); San Francisco Convention & Tourist Bureau; Redwood Empire Association; L.S. Starrett Company; British Metrication Board; John L. Chaney Instrument Corp.; Becton, Dickinson and Co.; Bausch & Lomb; Imperial Oil Limited (Canada)

Illustrations by Marjorie Wilson and Rebecca Lamm

Special thanks to Jeffrey V. Odom of the Metric Information Office who answered requests for information speedily and who also previewed my manuscript. I also wish to thank the design engineers who loaned me material and gave advice, especially Lowell Lemmons, James Scharnett and an engineer who grew up using the metric system. Egon Wolff.

Foreword

NOT MANY YEARS AGO many of the products made in foreign countries were considered very novel when offered for sale in the United States. We have now become quite accustomed to seeing and owning automobiles, cameras, shoes, and countless other products from many different countries. If you read the literature that comes with many of these products you will learn that size is usually described in millimeters or centimeters, weight in grams or kilograms and fluid volume in liters. Most countries use the metric system of measurement rather than our system of inches, pounds and gallons.

In the United States, we actually use both the metric system and our traditional system of inches, pounds, and gallons for measurement. Many Americans who are not familiar with the metric system think that it is used only by scientists and astronauts. Metric units, however, are used as the common measuring system in nearly every other major industrial country of the world except Canada, Australia, the United Kingdom and the United States. Except for the United States, these countries are now in the process of changing to the metric system and the United States is beginning to change also.

Many people in the United States ask why they should learn to use the metric system. There is really nothing wrong with inches, feet, ounces, pounds, gallons; so why change? As you read about the metric system in this book and learn to use it, I believe you will quickly understand why it is preferred by people in nearly all other countries of

7

the world. First of all, it is a much easier system to use and there is less chance for mistakes and misunderstandings. You do not have to remember unusual equivalents like: 12 inches equals one foot; 5280 feet equals one mile; 16 ounces equals one pound; 2000 pounds equals one ton. In metric the only number to remember is 10. It is a decimal system similar to our dollars and cents system for counting money. Second, and probably most important, if all countries of the world used the same measurement system it would simplify trade between countries.

In the years ahead you will probably have a chance to visit foreign countries. You might even have scientific or commercial dealings with them. Whatever your contact with people from abroad, you will find that a knowledge of the metric system will make things go much more smoothly.

Frank H. Winters
Director of Engineering
Caterpillar Tractor Company

4.8 cm

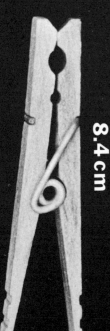

3.9 cm

19 cm

8.4 cm

15.6 cm

7.5 cm

4 cm

1. How High is High?

LISTEN! A jet is zooming overhead. It is leaving four thick trails of white smoke across the sky. How high is the jet from the ground?

There are many ways to answer this question.

You might look up at the plane and say, "The jet is very *high.*" However, a friend of yours might look at the same jet and say, "The plane is flying far *above* the clouds."

What does the word "high" or "above" mean?

Both of these words refer to the distance, called *height* or *altitude,* between the ground and the plane.

Many things around us have height. Mountains have height. So do buildings and many other things. But often we want to know just *how* high or tall the object is.

For example, a mountain climber likes to know how high the top of the mountain is above sea level, and a construction worker wants to know how high the top of a building is from the ground. These distances can be measured. To *measure* means to find the size or dimensions of an object, or the distance (space) between two points.

A building, of course, has more than height. A building also has *width* and *length.* *Width* is the distance of the short side of the building from end to end. *Length* is the distance of the long side of a building from end to end. When width, length, or height are measured, it is called *linear measurement.* The linear measurements of the height of a mountain, the width of a continent or the length of a river can be very long. The linear measurements of the sides of a postage stamp are, of course, very short.

This ski lift takes people up to the top of a high mountain in Switzerland. We have learned how to measure the *height* of the tallest mountains.

Linear measurement is probably used more often than any other type of measurement. But there are many other basic types of measurement, such as those for *weight* (heaviness of an object), or *volume* (space occupied by a substance, particularly a liquid).

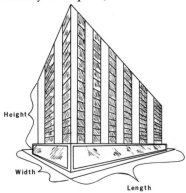

This drawing shows the three dimensions of a building: height, width and length.

Measurements of all types which tell us about the length, weight and volume of various objects are used every day. In order to make a television set, a chair, or even a toy, the manufacturer must first measure the parts that go into them. When meat, potatoes, milk and many other foods are sold to us they are measured by weight and volume and then we are charged for them. Clothes fit us because they have been measured. In fact, nearly everything people use, eat, or wear is measured in some way.

Most of your life, you have been measuring length or distance with inches and feet. And you have been weighing meat, potatoes and other things in ounces and pounds. These names given to common units of measure are known as the *customary system* in the United States. But these units of measurement are seldom used in other parts of the world.

In 1973, the United States, Canada, Britain and Australia were the only major industrial countries in the world that still measured length in inches and weight in pounds!

Don't they measure length and weight in other parts of the world? Of course they do, but most of the countries in the world use another measuring system called the *metric system*. The metric system does not use inches and pounds.

If you ever visit France or Denmark or Russia, you will discover that the height of buildings is measured in meters and centimeters instead of feet and inches. You would not

The National Aeronautics and Space Administration has used the metric system for all of its space flights and research programs. The camera, backpack and lunar scoop used here by Harrison Schmitt were all carefully weighed and measured in metric units before he left earth.

This "Moon Rover" was used to help astronauts explore the surface of the moon. If you watched the Rover in action on TV, you heard the astronauts refer to sizes and distances in metric units.

buy potatoes and meat by the pound. The store would sell them to you by the kilogram.

How does it happen that in one country distance is measured by inches and feet, while in another it is measured by meters? Just what is a measuring system? What is a meter? A kilogram?

These terms, and many other metric units, are becoming more and more important to the people of America every day. The United States will probably soon join the rest of the world and use the metric system for measuring. It is already being used by doctors, scientists and many engineers. American atheletes run, swim and ski Olympic events in meters. And our astronauts measure distance on the moon in meters and weigh their "gear" in kilograms.

In order to understand these units of measurement, and to learn why people in the United States are using them more and more everyday, let's go back and see how the use of measurement began.

In order to keep traffic moving freely along streets like this one in San Francisco, new ways of measuring traffic are constantly being developed.

2. Early Agriculture and Simple Measure

IN OUR MODERN CIVILIZATION, with cars, and trucks, and expressways, and busy schedules, measuring length, volume, weight, and even time is a constant necessity. But in the very earliest days of history, people had little need to know about length, weight or time.

More than 10,000 years ago, early man was a nomad, a wanderer. Much of his time and energy was spent merely trying to survive.

He didn't live in a permanent house in any one place. He followed the waterways in search of edible roots, berries, and wild animals. He fished the streams and camped where food was plentiful.

The daily life of these nomads and hunters was rather simple. They got up when the sun rose, and went to bed when darkness fell. As they followed the waterways, they did not ask, "How long is this stream?" Instead, they wondered if the stream had good water holes. At such places they were sure to find animals to hunt so that they would have fresh meat.

As they searched for food, they did not ask, "How far did I travel?" Neither did they wonder how big or small they were. It really didn't matter. The nomad didn't buy his clothing in a store. The animals he hunted did not come in sizes 12, 14, or 15½.

And how high was high? No one really cared. The sun in the sky gave light so men could hunt and fish. It didn't matter how far the sun was from the earth. They knew that from the clouds in the sky came rain, snow or sleet. But they did not wonder how high the clouds were above the trees. They were too busy trying to keep warm and dry.

Gradually, about 8,000 years ago, this simple, lonely nomadic way of life changed. Men and their families started to settle together in one area near some of the great rivers of the world. Many began to live in the eastern Mediterranean countries in the fertile valleys of the Tigris-Euphrates Rivers in Iraq. (The Babylonian civilization began in this area.) Others settled along the Nile in Egypt. Instead of wandering from place to place, they now began to build crude homes of dried mud, stone and logs. They began to plant crops and raise sheep, goats and other animals. They settled down and lived in *one* place. And this is how, nearly 5,000 years ago, some of the villages and cities—Thebes in Egypt, Baghdad and Babylon in Babylonia—of the Mediterranean region began.

As people began to farm the lands of the river valleys and build new dwellings, they made some interesting discoveries. If the logs they used to build animal pens and shelters were the same length, the pens and shelters were stronger. Their homes were more attractive and warmer (the wind didn't whistle through the cracks) if they chose stones and logs carefully.

Their homes were still simple, but they began to take on definite shapes and sizes. The parts were measured and were made to fit together. For the first time, the length of a log, and the size of an animal skin became important.

As settlements grew, individual families planted many of their crops close together. Now, it became important to have boundaries to separate each man's property from his neighbor's. At harvest time, each man wanted to know where his garden began and where his neighbor's ended.

And so, 4,000 to 5,000 years ago, settlers in the early villages and cities became more and more aware of the "long" and "short" of land and logs and streams. They

This carpenter is using a folding ruler to measure the framework of the house that he is building. Without exact measurement, precision building would be very difficult.

even started to keep a more accurate measure of seasons and yearly time. The use of measurement was just beginning, but these first simple uses had great influence on the units of measurement that are still being used today.

3. Early Formal Measurement

NO ONE KNOWS who was first to actually measure a log or limb or a section of land. It is known, though, that early man carried his "measuring stick" with him all the time. This may sound strange, but the truth is that man's own *body* was his first measuring rod!

How can you measure with your body? It's easy! First of all, remember, you don't use your entire body, just some of its parts, like an arm or leg. Without realizing it, so many of us still do it every day.

Have you been fishing lately? Perhaps you were lucky and caught a fish. How did you describe the size of the fish to your family or friends? In inches? Pounds? Probably not. Most likely you held up your two hands and said, "You should have seen the fish I caught! It was that long!"

There are several ways of using your body to measure. If someone asks, "How tall is your brother?" you can answer, "Oh, he comes to here on me," and point to your shoulder. When you talk about the huge wave that knocked you down last summer on the beach, you can tell your friends, "It was this high!" and raise your hand far above your head. And so, in the same way, our ancestors used parts of their bodies to indicate size and shape.

The first use of the body to measure lengths and widths was for more practical purposes than describing the size of a fish or a wave. Man used hand and foot measurements to make life easier and more orderly. He marked off land with his feet, by "stepping it off," as is often done today when we estimate distances, and he used his hands and arms to measure logs for his home.

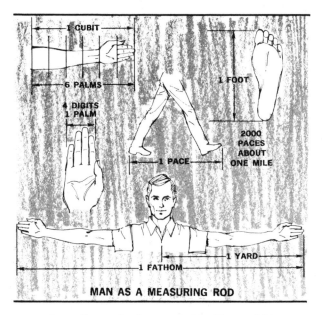

MAN AS A MEASURING ROD

Man himself was the first yardstick. He used his own body to measure the height, width, and length of objects, and the distance between places.

Later, many of these body measurements were given specific names.

The length of a man's foot became known as a *foot*.

The length of a man's step or stride, measured from the heel of one foot to the toe of the other, was known as a *pace*.

A *fathom* was the distance between the fingertips of a man's two outstretched arms. Today, a fathom (which is equal to six feet) is still used by many seamen to measure the depth of water.

The width of a finger, used to measure small items, became known as a *digit*. Although we don't hear about the digit too much anymore, it was similar to the use of an inch in today's measurements.

One of the oldest units of measure that made use of the arm was the *cubit*. It dates back several thousand years. The exact length of the ancient cubit is not known.

This is an artist's idea of how the early Egyptians measured the huge blocks of stone which were used in building the pyramids. The *cubit* was the unit of measurement used by the early Egyptians.

However, the Royal Egyptian cubit is usually described as "the length of a man's arm from the elbow to the end of the outstretched middle finger." Three to four thousand years ago, Egyptians used the cubit to build huge temples and massive pyramids.

There are passages in the Bible referring to the cubit. Noah's Ark, the Ark of the Covenant, and Solomon's Temple were measured in cubits.

The cubit was useful to many of the early Mediterranean civilizations. Historians and archeologists have evidence that the Greeks and Romans constructed many of their buildings in Rome and Athens 2,500 years ago using the cubit as their basis for measurement. The cubit used by the Greeks and Romans, which became known as the Olympic cubit, was slightly shorter than the ancient Egyptian cubit. The Olympic cubit was usually known as the length of a man's forearm *from his wrist to his elbow*, instead of *from the elbow to the tip of the middle finger.*

The fathom and the cubit were just two of the early measurements that made use of the length of a man's arm. The arm was also used to measure lengths of cloth. In many markets, the practice of pulling materials around the bent elbow was a method used to measure cloth. This unit of measure was called an *ell*.

Ell may be a shortened form of the word "elbow." An ell was the length of material that would stretch from a merchant's hand, around his bent arm and to his shoulder.

(The ell was very similar in length to the English yard. As we will see later, however, the English yard was measured along an outstretched arm rather than around a bent elbow.)

Let's take an imaginary trip back into time—about 600 years back—and see how this measurement, the ell, was used. Watch a buyer in the marketplace of Venice (Italy) or Alexandria (Egypt)—two Mediterranean trading centers. The buyer studies the bolts of material spread out before him. He studies the fabrics carefully before making a decision.

"I want this blue cloth," he says.

"Yes, yes," the merchant says eagerly. "How many ell do you want?" he asks.

"Ten," the buyer replies, and the merchant pulls the blue material along his arm, around his elbow ten times.

In just this manner, the ell was used for centuries by merchants selling silks, linens and other types of woven materials. Believe it or not, in some of the remote areas of India and Africa, the ell is still being used today.

So, as we see, for many years the simple measurement of length and width were all that man needed. But, in time, trade between cities became more important. Men began to buy and sell copper, gold, silver and other precious metals, and new problems arose.

How do you measure a valuable piece of gold or silver accurately? Certainly not with your foot or your hand. It was necessary to find a more exact type of measurement. This new measurement was called *weight*.

Measuring the weights of precious metals and other

This type of balance was used by the early Egyptians and is still used by some jewelers and pharmacists today. The weights in front of the scale are metric.

small items dates far back to the ancient civilizations of Mesopotamia and Egypt. Archeologists have found weights made of limestone in the ruins of both of these early areas. Papyrus records have been found that show that Egyptians used balances and weights more than 6,000 years ago.

The Egypitan balances, which were quite similar to those used by some jewelers and pharmacists today, were simple but efficient. They had two small pans hanging from the ends of a horizontal bar that was supported in the middle by a vertical bar. If equal amounts of weight were placed in each of the shallow pans, the horizontal bar was level, and the pans balanced each other.

The weights that were placed in the pans of the ancient balances were usually made of stone or precious metals, such as gold and silver. But other types were also used.

In Mesopotamia, the *mina* and the *talent* were used. The mina and the talent were used as money as well as measuring units. In some Mediterranean countries, the Roman *libra* and the *uncia* were used as weights. The libra and uncia (twelve unciae equaled one libra) were used in all regions of the Mediterranean for a few hundred years, and became the basis for the modern *pound* (libra) and *ounce* (uncia).

Measurement of length and weight were the oldest units of the measuring system developed in the countries that bordered the Mediterranean Sea. But, as Egyptian, Roman and Greek ships began to sail more and more frequently from shore to shore, and even out into the Atlantic, they carried such food products as olive oil, wine and grapes which could not be measured as conveniently as a log, or a building block. In other words, they could not be measured in units of length, width and height. Nor could they be weighed on a balance. A new kind of measurement was needed and soon merchants began to use a type of measure called *volume*.

Volume, as we mention in Chapter One, is the space occupied by a substance. And the amount of space occupied depends on the size (length, width and height) of the container.

In early times, volume was measured in just this way. The Babylonians used a container for this puipose. They would describe a container as being "one handbreadth high, one handbreadth wide and one handbreadth long," and everyone would know the volume of the product in the container.

Not all containers were alike in size or were made of the same materials. Pottery jugs of various sizes and shapes were used to sell olive oil and other liquids. Rye, barley and wheat were often sold in stone jars. After a while, jars were used only for liquids, and grains were sold in reed baskets. In fact, the use of the reed basket became quite popular for grain and other bulky items and this was probably the way in which the "bushel" basket was first used.

For several hundred years, all of the various types of measurement developed by the Egyptians, Romans and Greeks were used only in the Mediterranean countries.° But, as early as the first century, the measuring system of these countries was spread by explorers and trading ships into the lands that are now known as France, Germany and Great Britain.

°Countries in the Far East—China, Japan, and India—also developed a measuring system during these early centuries. These units of measurement are not discussed in this book because they had very little to do with the development of the metric system or the U.S. customary system.

4. How Long Is a Foot?

UP UNTIL THE YEAR 1,000, trade spread rather slowly through the major countries of Europe. The need for exact measurement was, therefore, not too important.

After the tenth century, however, trade between France, Germany and Great Britain began to expand and the need for more accurate types of measurement became increasingly important to businessmen. People came to realize that the units of length, weight, and volume varied too much from one country to the next. A uniform method of measuring length and weight was needed. Otherwise, how could countries carry on business with each other?

The years between 1100 and 1600 were a period of rapid growth. Cities in the Mediterranean such as Alexandria, Constantinople and Carthage were growing. Cordova and Seville (in Spain) and Paris were also becoming centers of industry and commerce. Other cities—such as Genoa, Venice, Lisbon and London—were becoming important seaports and centers of trade. Ships sailed frequently in and out of these seaports.

Many countries were also exploring farther and farther along the coast of Africa in search of a water route to the orient. Finally, a breakthrough came when, in the 1480's and 1490's, Vasco da Gama and Bartholomew Diaz ventured safely around the Cape of Good Hope (on the tip of Africa) while Christopher Columbus sailed safely across the Atlantic and back in 1492. These men and their crews proved that the world did not end just over the horizon.

Suddenly, interest in measurement grew greater and greater. Explorers wanted to know more about the sizes and shapes of the oceans. Merchants wanted to know the exact distance between the new ports that had been discovered so they could make plans to buy and sell in the new countries.

In the 1500's, explorers and merchants were not the only ones who were looking over the horizon. This period of history, called the Renaissance, was a time of curiosity about many things.

Scientists and astronomers began to wonder what the earth and the universe really looked like. Two famous astronomers of the late 1500's—Tycho Brahe from Denmark and Johann Kepler from Germany—began to study the paths of stars, planets and comets. And, with the aid of a new invention, the telescope, an Italian, Galileo Galilei, spent many sleepless nights in the year 1610 studying the sky.

Amazing! Galileo observed. The moon is not smooth. It is wrinkled and pitted. Deep valleys are hidden in dark shadows. But mountain ridges are bright with sunlight. And those clouds in the milky way are really stars! Millions and millions of stars.

In the year 1620, still another invention, the microscope, helped another Italian, Marcello Malphighi, see the tiny blood vessels in the human body. Later in the seventeenth century, Anton van Leeuwenhoek, a janitor living in Delft, Holland, started an unusual hobby. He began to make microscopes! In fact, by the year 1673, he had built 247 of them.

Anton van Leeuwenhoek was fascinated by the lenses of his microscopes, and what he could see through them. A drop of his own blood was full of tiny particles. A single drop of water was squirming with thousands of *living* creatures!

So, the telescope enabled people to see far out into space,

and the microscope enabled them to see tiny, tiny things. The meaning of the words "small" and "large" had greatly changed. The use of measurement *had* to become more efficient and accurate so that men could intelligently describe the many things they studied.

Fortunately, the increased importance and need for better measurements led to a problem that actually helped develop a more accurate measuring system, not only for scientists and merchants, but for all people.

As settlements grew into cities, and trade spread from Spain, Portugal and England to all parts of the world, local methods of measuring grain, cloth, and land were questioned. The *foot* was based on the size of a man's foot! But, are all men's feet the same size?

Just imagine that you are buying a section of land 100 feet long. Who would you ask to "step it off," a tall man with a long, thin foot or a small man with a short, stubby foot? Naturally, you would ask the tall man. But, what if the seller insists that the short man's foot is really a true foot? Now you have a problem. *Just how long is a foot?*

The same problem came up in measuring lengths of cloth and baskets of grain. Too often, the length of a foot used to measure lumber or cloth in France was not the same size as the foot used in Spain. A basket or a bushel of wheat sold on the coast of Italy was not the same as a basket or a bushel of wheat sold in a small town 50 miles away.

Things were confused. Merchants, scientists and craftsmen wanted a measuring system that had units of length and weight that were equal and could be compared. It became obvious that a set of *standards* was needed.

Standards are measurement units set up as a rule or model to follow. They must always be the same, they cannot change. To "standarize" or to be "standard" means to have uniform size or to be equal in dimensions. Today, we give standard measurement very little thought because we have rulers, yardsticks, and measuring tapes that are always the same. A 12-inch ruler in New York or Michigan is the same length as a 12-inch ruler in California, or any other state, because they were made according to a standard model. But, craftsmen and scientists of the thirteenth and fourteenth centuries had no models or standards to follow.

The first models or standards were set up only in individual guilds or cities. However, eventually, standards had to be set up for entire countries. These were usually decided upon by the leader or king.

Many of the early standards for everyday measuring units used in the United States today were decreed, or established, by English kings. For example, the early measure of a yard or "gird" (a Saxon word referring to the size or length of a person's waist°) is believed to have been set by King Henry I. In the 1100's, King Henry I measured the distance from the tip of his nose to the thumb of his outstretched hand. "This length," he delcared, "will henceforth be known as a *yard*." And, by the 1300's, written records of England listed other official lengths. An *inch* in 1324 was to be "the length of threé barley corns, round and dry, taken from the center of the ear and laid end to end." The *foot* was *twelve inches*. Later, in the 1500's, King Henry VIII decreed that the standard yard was *three feet*, and he even had this measure marked on a bronze yard bar. This, as you may have guessed, is the origin of the *yardstick*.

During the same period when merchants and kings were concerned with standards for measuring length and width, they were also trying to develop standards for measuring liquids and grains. Just how big was a bushel or a basket of

---

°The use of a yard as a measure for length dates back to early Saxon kings who wore a sash or girdle around their waist. This "gird" could be removed to measure lengths of various items.

The apples above are sold in bushel baskets. The *bushel* is not an exact measurement. Some baskets are piled high, and some are not.

wheat or rye? Should you "heap" the grain or leave it "flat?" What size containers should be used?

The same was true for ounces and pounds. Standards for weights were needed, too. King Edward, who was King of England from 1272 to 1307, helped set up some standards for weight in his country.

But, still, a big problem remained. Who was to decide these standards in other countries? An Englishman *sold* cloth by the yard, but in some countries he *bought* it by the ell. A bushel of grain bought from a farmer on the plateau lands in central Spain was not the same as a bushel sold in Liverpool or London. Things were confusing!

Unfortunately, many of the merchants and tradesmen were not too concerned. They struggled along with their old "mixed methods" because that was all they had ever known.

Remember, however, that this was a time of great learning in many fields. Some merchants were willing to struggle along with the old methods, but many merchants, scientists, and educators were not satisfied. They wanted a set of measurements that were not based on long or short feet, or a king's arm. They wanted accurate, efficient ways to measure tiny particles of water or even air, as well as large sections of land. In short, people found that the standards that had been developed so far were not good enough.

It wasn't long before the need was taken very seriously, and the first steps were taken that led to a system that is used today in most of the world.

5. The French Invent the Meter

THE BIRTH OF the metric system took place in France. In the late 1700's, France was a country in which peasants on the farms and workers in the cities were rebelling against a monarchy (a government ruled by a king) that was treating them unfairly. France was also busily engaged in another kind of revolution—a revolution of learning and progress.

The leaders and educators of France were busy experimenting with new methods of education and research. Because of all these activities and the new discoveries they produced, French scientists wanted to have new standards of measurement established. They found that the old system of measurement was not good enough.

In May of 1790, the National Assembly of France asked the Paris Academy of Science to appoint a commission to develop a complete set of new units of measurement. As a result, the Academy appointed Jean Charles Borda, Pierre La Place, Gaspard Monge and Antoine Lavoisier—all French scientists.

There were many problems with the old system, but setting up a new one was not easy. The men on the commission spent many hours in research and discussions.

"The new system must be efficient," some members of the commission said.

"Yes," others remarked, "the new units of measurement must be easy to use, but they must also be very accurate."

"And we can't use units of measure based on a man's arm or foot. They must be units that do not change."

For almost nine long years, the discussions went on and on. At first, the scientists and other members of the commission talked mostly about the measurement of length, or *linear measure*. Later, they also studied the old cubits, fathoms, yards, and feet. These familiar units were important in every person's life, but could not always be used very efficiently.

The commission members were trying to find a unit of basic measure that is common to *all* people in all parts of the world; one that was easy to use for merchants and tradesmen as well as scientists.

Several ideas were discussed. The men could not agree. Then, one day, one of the men suggested, "Why not use the earth itself as the basic unit of measurement?"

At first there was some disbelief. Did the men hear correctly? Use the earth as a basic unit for measurement!

After careful study, the commission agreed that using the earth was a very good idea. After all, two French scientists, Jacques Cassini and Nicholas L. de Lacaille, had already experimented in the past century with measuring the arc, or curve, of the earth. The commission had some facts with which to begin. And so, with great excitement, the commission plunged into the work that was cut out for them.

But, the earth is very big, isn't it? How can the earth be used to help measure land, lumber and pieces of machinery?

The answer isn't as complicated as you might think. Look at a globe or a map. The globe is divided by two sets of lines. One set of lines, called *parallels of latitude*, circles the world from east to west. Parallels measure distance in degrees, north and south of the equator. The other set of lines goes around the world up and down, from north to south, from pole to pole. They are called *meridians of longitude*. Meridians measure or divide the earth by degrees east and west of the Prime Meridian which runs through Greenwich, England.

Parallels and meridians had been used for centuries before the French commission met in 1790. They were proven to be quite reliable and accurate. In Chapter One, we discussed "measure" and said it described the size or dimensions of an object. To measure accurately means to compare the object being measured with a known standard. Parallels and meridians, and the degrees of measurement that they represented, were accurate divisions of the earth. The commission decided that a meridian *could* be used as a standard or model for their new measuring system.

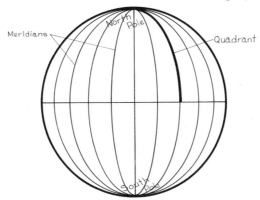

Meridians divide the earth by degrees east and west of the Prime Meridian. A *quadrant* is one-fourth of a meridian.

But, a meridian is very long. If you could fly above the meridian that goes through your home town, you could follow it around the entire earth. For example, board a plane in St. Louis, Missouri, and fly south over the 90th meridian. A few hours after you leave the airport, you will see the Gulf of Mexico, the Yucatan peninsula and Guatemala. Soon, you cross the equator and have a long, long flight over the Pacific until you come to the frozen lands of Antarctica.

After a while, without changing its course, the plane is suddenly flying you *north*! It takes you over the Indian Ocean, and across the equator again. You have flown more than half-way around the world!

The plane continues its flight. It takes you over the center of the continent of Asia and over the North Pole. Then you realize that you are flying south again! South to the United States and St. Louis, the place where your journey began. All this time, you have been flying over a meridian.

Since meridians are so very long, the French commission didn't use the entire length of a meridian as its standard. They used just one of its sections. On your imaginary trip around the circumference of the world, the plane passed over several key points—the equator, and the North and South poles. These key points divide a meridian into four parts or *quadrants*. The quadrant became the section of a meridian that the commission used as the basis for its measuring system.

On a map, they drew an imaginary line through Paris— along the meridian, 2.23° E, that runs from the North Pole

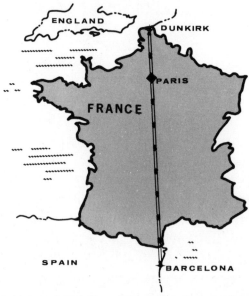

Dunkirk, Paris and Barcelona all lie on the same meridian. By measuring this distance, astronomers were able to calculate the length of a quadrant of a meridian.

to the equator. They chose this particular meridian for two reasons. First, this meridian ran directly through France between Dunkirk on the north coast and Mont Jany on the south coast (near Barcelona). Second, they already knew the latitude (degrees north of the equator) of both of these two towns and knew there were approximately 8 degrees in this section of the meridian. If they could accurately measure the distance *over land* between the two towns, they could figure the distance or length of one degree.

For example, if the distance on land is 544 miles for eight degrees, then the distance of one degree is 544 divided by 8, or 68 miles.

After they knew the distance of one degree, they could calculate the distance or length of 90 degrees (number of degrees in a quadrant). If one degree = 68 miles, then a quadrant or 90 degrees = 90 x 6, or 6120 miles. (Remember, these are approximate figures. The commission used exact measurements for their calculations.)

The commission asked two French astronomers, Pierre F.A. Mechain and Jean Baptiste Delambre, to measure and calculate the exact length of the quadrant. It was a difficult task. But after seven years and many hardships, the two astronomers were able to report back to the commission with the measurement of the quadrant.

"We will divide this distance into *ten million* parts," the commission said. "We will use the length of *one* part as our *basic unit.*"

The commission called this basic unit a *metron* or *meter.*° (Metron is a Greek word that means "measure.") The meter was then divided into ten equal parts. Since the commission had used a Greek word for the basic unit

---

°The French word for this unit of measurement is *metre*. However, in this book we will use the spelling recommended by the National Bureau of Standards.

(meter), they again turned to the Greek language for a name for the ten smaller units.

"*Deci* means ten," one of the members of the commission said. "Let's call the ten smaller units *decimeters.*"

They did just that and decided to use Greek prefixes for units smaller than a decimeter. The meter was divided into one hundred parts and each unit was named a *centimeter.* They also divided the meter into a thousand equal parts and called them *millimeters.*

Greek prefixes were also used for units of length that were larger than a meter. *Deca* is the Greek for ten. Therefore, the distance across a field that was ten meters long became a *decameter.* In the same way, a hundred meters became a *hectometer.* Distances between towns that were one thousand meters or more were called *kilometers.*

By the time the commission had begun naming the units of their new system, the system itself also had a name. It became known as the *metric system.* But, it also had another name. It was often referred to as the *decimal measuring system* because the larger and smaller units of the basic meter were created by multiplying or dividing by 10 or by miltiples of 10 (100, 1,000, etc.). You will see in the following chapters how the measurements of the decimal or metric system are used, and also how they compare to units with which you are familiar.

What is most important to remember now is that the new metric system used centimeters and millimeters to measure small objects. It used meters and kilometers to measure highways and distances across countries. The meter was very useful in measuring length and width. But this did not solve all problems.

What about food products or bulky items that needed to be weighed, or liquids that were sold in containers? How did the French use a quadrant (one ten-millionth of the earth) to measure corn or sugar or milk?

6. Weighing a Cube of Water

WEIGHING A GOLD NUGGET, a sack of salt, or a bag of flour was not new to the French scientists. Merchants had been weighing products (wheat, corn, flax, oats, mineral ores, etc.) for hundreds of years.

In the 1790's, the most commonly accepted units for measuring weight were the ounce and the pound. This method, however, was often not a very good system to follow because a pound of flour or oats in Rome was equal to twelve ounces, while a pound of flour or oats in London was equal to sixteen ounces.

The members of the French commission decided not to use any of the old units to weigh solid objects because they did not have an accurate standard of weight.

That was certainly true. It was difficult to decide how much an ounce should be; it varied from one country to another. They realized that because a pound was made up of ounces, they had to know exactly what an ounce was; otherwise, how could they know when a pound was a pound. (In many cities, the inch and the yard were causing the same confusion as the ounce and the pound.)

The French scientists were determined to develop a totally new system of weights and measures, and the new unit of weight would have to be based in some way on the *meter*.

So, the metric committee asked a very well-known scientist, Antoine Laurent Lavoisier, to help them. Lavoisier had often experimented with scales and balances and, in his research, he had worked with many different substances. They asked him to begin experimenting with weighing a *cube* of water.

A cube of water! You know what water is, but do you know what a cube is? A cube is like a box. It has four sides, a bottom, and a top. Probably the most common cube everyone has seen and even played with is an alphabet block. All sides on the block are exactly the same size. The top is the same size as the bottom, and the top and bottom are the very same size on all four sides. If you roll the block over, the sides will look just like the top and the top will look like the sides. The *dimensions* of each side are equal. The *equal* size of all sides is what makes a cube a cube!

The cube that Lavoisier experimented with was quite small. Its height, length and width were each a small unit of the meter. He used a cube that was one centimeter high, one centimeter wide, and one centimeter long. (A cube of this size is called a *cubic centimeter*.)

But Lavoisier did not use a solid cube like the alphabet block. Instead, he used a hollow cube that could be filled with water. Nor did he use ordinary water. He wanted his cubic centimeter of water to be a standard that could be checked for accuracy.

So, in his experiments, Lavoisier used pure, or *distilled*, water that had a temperature that was just above freezing. The weight of this cubic centimeter of water became the basic unit of weight for the metric system. The French called the new unit of weight, a *gram*.

After agreeing upon the weight and the name for this first unit of weight, measuring and naming larger and smaller units was easy. The same prefixes that had been used for the meter (the unit of *length*), were used for the gram. Small units of weight were named *centigrams* (centigrams—one-hundredth of a gram) and *milligrams* (milligrams—one-thousandth of a gram). Larger units were

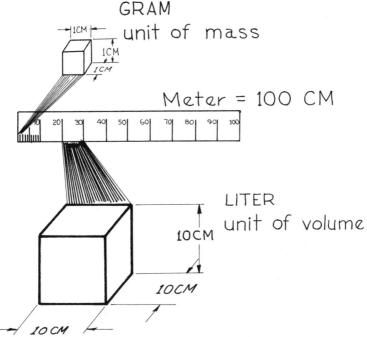

GRAM
unit of mass

Meter = 100 CM

LITER
unit of volume

The above drawing shows us that the units of measurement for weight and volume in the metric system are based on the meter-measuring unit for length. The gram became the weight (or mass) of water contained in a cube 1 centimeter x 1 centimeter x 1 centimeter. The liter became the amount of liquid which could fit into a container 10 centimeters x 10 centimeters x 10 centimeters.

named *kilograms* (kilo-grams—one-thousand grams). One million grams were named *megagrams* or a *metric ton*.

The gram was useful for weighing or measuring salt, corn and other solid objects. But what about fluids or liquids such as milk, oil or wine? The French knew that liquids could be measured by weight, but found that it would be better if they were measured by *volume*—by the amount of space they occupy. How could they accomplish this?

Again, the metric committee used a cube. However, the *space* needed for *fluid volume* is larger than the space needed for solid objects of the same weight. So, the cube used for volume had to be larger than the cube used for weight. This time, the scientists used a hollow cube that was one decimeter (one-tenth of a meter) high, one decimeter wide and one decimeter long. The cube was filled to the brim with water. This cubic decimeter—the amount that could fit into a cube of one decimeter by one decimeter by one decimeter—was called a *liter*. And just like the meter and the gram, the liter had larger and smaller units: the *deciliter* (deci-liter), *milliliter* (milli-liter) and *kiloliter* (kilo-liter). We will learn more about them and how they are used in a later chapter.

The most important task of the French commission was now finished. They had invented:

1. a meter to measure length,
2. a gram to measure weight,
3. a liter to measure liquid volume (or capacity).

Naming and defining these basic units of measurement —meter, gram, and liter—was just the first step in establishing the metric system. Now the units had to be put to work.

7. Early Use of the Meter in France

HAVING A GOOD measurement system and putting the system to good use were two different matters. The French commission believed their new system of weights and measures was superior to the old system, and that the people of France would adopt the new units immediately. But, merchants, farmers and students do not change their ways easily. The early years of the metric system (1793-1800) were filled with great confusion. These last years of the eighteenth century in France were filled with fear. Those who rebelled against the government were led to the guillotine where their heads were cut off. In such times, it was difficult to carry on normal trade and industry.

Frenchmen living in the major cities of France, and particularly in Paris, lived in constant fear of the guillotine, while peasants feared death by starvation. Such people were not concerned with the meter. They were concerned with staying alive.

Buying milk in *any* quantity was more important than asking for it by the liter. Running a shoe shop in Paris without being arrested was more important than measuring leather for shoes in centimeters. Despite these difficulties, and despite its slow growth, the French commission was not discouraged and kept up its work on the metric system.

In 1795, they set up a conference in Paris to discuss their new decimal system. Representatives of Great Britain and other countries were invited to attend this meeting. One important decision that grew out of this conference was to construct a *standard meter bar* and a *standard kilogram*.

The French intended for the meter bar, or *metre des archives*, as they called it, to be a standard for the world, not just for France.

This first meter bar and kilogram were very carefully measured and molded out of platinum. In 1799, they were placed on display in special cases in the Academy of Science.

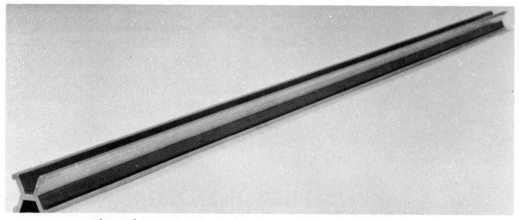

This is the prototype meter bar kept at the International Bureau of Weights and Measures in France. Exact duplicates of this bar were given to every government represented at the bureau.

In 1801, the National Assembly passed a law declaring the metric decimal system to be compulsory. They also decided that copies of the meter bar and kilogram would be produced, and would be used as national standards in all of the cities in France.

But the government did not have enough money to make standards for all of the cities, and, for several years, merchants used their own measurements of the meter and kilogram. Many, of course, were not accurate.

For almost ten years, the metric decimal system was used rather haphazardly in France. Scientists and some merchants accepted it readily, but, in many sections of the country, the new units were not used at all or were used at the same time that the old measuring units were being used.

In 1812, the very existence of the new system was threatened. Napoleon, who was Emperor of France at that time, issued a decree saying that the law of 1801, which created the metric system, did not have to be obeyed. Fortunately, the decree did not abolish the new system or say that it could *not* be used. But, it *did* officially restore the old units of measure. As you can imagine, during the next few years, measurement was more confusing than ever for the French people.

In spite of all of this confusion, it is rather surprising and significant that the use of the meter and gram gradually became more popular than the old units of length and weight. The new system was being put to use by more and more people.

Three factors helped make the metric system popular. First, in about the year 1815, the economy of France began to change. The change was slow. Order was restored all over the country and the people felt at peace. Farmers in Normandy were able to plow their fields and sell their crops of wheat, apples and sugar beets without fear. The factories of Lille and Lyon began to produce fine cottons and linens again. The port of Rouen was teeming with dock-hands loading and unloading cargo.

The second factor that helped the metric system become popular was that French schools and universities began to teach the metric units.

Thirdly, in 1837, when the metric system was nearly 40 years old, the French government took a decisive step in making certain that all French citizens used the meter, liter and gram. The Chamber of Deputies and the Chamber of Peers passed a law proclaiming that after January 4, 1840 the decimal metric system *had to be used* in every store, factory and school. The main provisions of this law said that:

1. The decree of February 12, 1812, concerning weights

and measures, is repealed.

2. The use of all other instruments for weighing and measuring that were made in accordance with the law of 1812, will not be permitted after January 1, 1840.

3. After January 1, 1840 all weights and measures, other than those of the decimal metric system, shall be forbidden under penalties.

4. Anyone having in his possession weights and measures that did not conform to the metric system would be punished.

So, after 1840, the metric system became the official measuring system of France. It wasn't exactly a smashing success in its mother country, but it was becoming familiar to more and more Frenchmen. And, gradually, it was even adopted in other European countries.

8. Great Britain and the U.S. Reject the Metric Units

THE METRIC SYSTEM, as we have seen, had a stormy beginning in France. Before long, however, the liter, meter and gram became more and more popular in Belgium and the Netherlands—countries which traded frequently with France.

Most countries, however, did not like the metric system. In fact, in the late 1790's and early 1800's, many people in various parts of the world were opposed to *anything* that was French.

France's neighbor, Great Britain, a short distance across the English Channel, was one of those countries. France and Great Britain had been enemies for many years. A member of the Royal Society of London (a British scientific organization) called the new French units, "complicated, worthless barbarisms."

"We need a new set of standards, but they must be sensible," the British said. "They must be similar to the old units established by our kings so that people will know how to use them." So, Great Britain kept her familiar units of yards, inches, and pounds.

But, holding on to the old system of measurement was to lead to many problems for Britain. She had a vast empire, with colonies in Asia, Africa, and North America. Very few of the merchants in her colonies used the same system of yards, inches and pounds that the English merchants in London, Manchester or Southampton used.

In 1824, Great Britain did set up better standards for her yard and gallon. The new standards were known as *imperial* units. During those years when France and some of her European neighbors were learning to use the metric system, Britain and her colonies were using the imperial system.

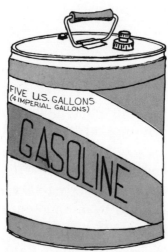

Both the United States and Britain have measured liquid volume in gallons for many years. However, the British imperial gallon is larger than the United States gallon. Four imperial gallons equal five United States gallon.

The metric units, however, were not completely ignored in Great Britain. As in other countries, scientists and technicians who depended on very accurate measurements began to use the decimal system in their research and in the execution of their research. But most Englishmen used the imperial system.

The metric system was received in the new nation called the United States of America in much the same way as it was in Great Britain. But for a different reason!

In the 1790's, when the metric system was just being developed, the United States was not yet a real nation. It consisted of a mere 13 states trying to find a way to work together. Statesmen, merchants, farmers and explorers in various cities and territories of the country were faced with many different problems. Neither the statesmen, the farmers nor the pioneers were very interested in adopting a new set of measurements. Many were not even aware that a measurement known as a meter or gram existed.

A few Americans did know about the metric system, however. Men like Thomas Jefferson, John Quincy Adams, and other early leaders knew about these measuring units and realized how important such standards could be for a growing nation. They tried to get the first United States Congress to establish standards for both measurement and money. Congress did vote on a money system, the system which is still used today, but Congress could not agree on standards for length and weight.

For years, the yard, pound and bushel were used in the United States without any government standards. Finally, in the 1830's, the U.S. Senate appointed the U.S. Coast Survey Office, under the supervision of the Secretary of the Treasury, to make a study of weights and measures used in the states. The study revealed that the use of weights and measures varied from state to state. So, the Secretary of the Treasury, Louis McLane, asked the Coast Survey Office to furnish each state with uniform and accurate weights and measures. These weights and measures were based on the yard, an avoirdupois pound and a bushel. They were the beginning of the measuring system that became known as the U.S. customary system.

So, by the time the metric system was compulsory in France (1840), there were three measuring systems being used in Europe and North America—the imperial system, the U.S. customary system, and the metric system. Only one—the metric system—was spreading rapidly.

9. The Metric System Circles the Globe

EVEN THOUGH the United States and Britain did not readily accept the metric system, there were many countries that began to use meters, liters, and grams voluntarily as a standard of measurement. France's neighbors were the first countries to make the change.

Merchants in Belgium, Luxembourg and the Netherlands sold coal, linen and dairy products to the French. In return, they bought wheat, iron ore and lumber. They watched the French merchants weigh their products in grams and kilograms and measure cloth in meters. They soon realized that the French units were easier to use than those of their own countries. Soon, Luxembourg, Belgium and the Netherlands began using the decimal system. By 1840, the year in which the metric system became compulsory in France, all three of these countries had officially adopted the metric units of weight and measurement.

Soon thereafter, the new system spread very rapidly. In fact, within 40 years, nearly every country in Europe, including Germany, Switzerland, Austria, Italy and Spain had adopted the metric system.

Merchants and colonists from these countries took the metric system into the cities of Africa and South America. By 1880, the meter had come into common usage in Algeria, Peru, Chile and Bolivia. The metric system's growth between 1800 and 1880 was truly incredible!

The French system had proven itself! It had spread faster and farther in just a few decades than the inch-pound units had spread in several centuries. Of course, we must

France   Belgium
Netherlands   Luxembourg
Switzerland   Algeria
Hungary   Portugal
Brazil   Monaco
Peru   Italy
Spain   Chile
Austria   Bolivia
Colombia   Ecuador
Liechtenstein   Germany
Czechoslovakia
Mauritius

THE METRIC WORLD OF 1880

This map shows the nations of the world using the metric system in 1880.

remember that the inch-pound system had struggled through a period of history during which transportation was slow and trade was limited to a small area of the world. The metric system, on the other hand, came into being at a time when industry and the use of machinery was increasing rapidly in all countries of the world, and ships could sail *around* the world in less time than Columbus had taken to cross the Atlantic.

Another reason the metric units spread so quickly was that, as the French had predicted, it was an easy system to learn and use because the units were *decimal* units. Just what does this mean? Why had the French used the decimal system for their weights and measurements?

The prefix *deci* means "ten." The decimal metric system is based on the number ten. The basic unit, the meter, was one *ten* millionth of a quadrant. The smaller units were created by dividing the meter by 10 and then by 100 and

1,000. Larger units were created by multiplying by 10, 100, and 1,000. The inch-pound units were based on numbers like 12, 16, and 36. How much simpler to use 10, 100, and 1,000! It is easier and quicker to multiply 352 by 10 than to multiply 352 by 12.

The use of a "base ten" (or decimal) system was not new when the metric system was being developed. The Chinese and Babylonians had used a decimal counting system long before 1790. And many countries in the 1700's used a decimal system for counting money. It was logical and simple for these countries to learn the metric system after they understood the basic units. In fact, the decimal metric units were so logical that, as we have seen, they were used on nearly every continent of the world in less than 200 years.

Because the metric system was accepted by so many countries in the 1860's, many scientists, engineers and political leaders felt it was important to establish some kind of international committee on weights and measurements. As a result, in 1869, delegates from 17 nations met in Paris to discuss international standards for weight and length.

This Metric Convention held several sessions during the next six years and it was the first of a series of more than a dozen important international conferences. Weights and measures had now become of worldwide interest and concern.

10. The Treaty of the Meter

UNFORTUNATELY, THE FIRST International Conference had a very poor beginning. Just as the meetings were beginning, war was declared, in August, 1870, between France and Prussia (a kingdom at that time in northern Germany). So, the sessions were cancelled.

This Franco-Prussian War did not last long, however, and in September of 1872 the delegates again came to Paris. Meetings resumed, and delegates from 20 countries —United States, Germany, Austria-Hungary, Belgium, Brazil, Argentine Confederation, Denmark, Spain, France, Italy, Peru, Portugal, Russia, Sweden, Norway, Switzerland, Turkey, Venezuela, Holland, and Great Britain— spent the next three years discussing international problems of measurement.

The discussions covered many topics. Two of the important recommendations which resulted from the meetings were that a new international meter bar be constructed, and that an International Bureau of Weights and Measures be established. The Bureau was to be supported by all nations who agreed to the proposal.

In May of 1875, the meetings ended, and delegates from 17 countries, including the United States, signed the Treaty of the Meter. The treaty officially incorporated many of the resolutions adopted by the Convention, including proposals to construct a new meter bar, and to establish an International Bureau.

Very carefully, a *prototype* (an original model) of a meter bar and a kilogram weight were constructed out of

This photo shows how well the prototype kilogram kept at the International Bureau in France is protected. If the weight must be removed, the special tongs shown are used.

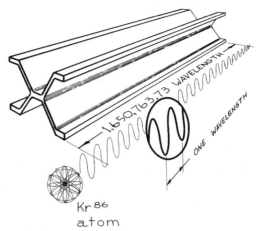

Kr 86
atom

Though a platinum-iridium meter bar is still kept at the International Bureau of Weights and Measures, today scientists also measure the meter with minute light wave lengths of Krypton 86.

platinum and iridium. The Metric Convention of 1875 had decided to use a combination of platinum and iridium in making the new standard meter bar and kilogram weight because these ores do not expand or contract easily. They can be packed in ice, or heated in boiling water without change in their size and shape.

When the prototype bar and kilogram were finished, in 1889, they were placed in the headquarters of the new International Bureau of Weights and Measures. The headquarters of the International Bureau was built on the banks of the river Seine, near Sevres, France. The Bureau is located there to this day.

Another wise decision of the Metric Convention was to set up guidelines for future international conferences that might be called from time to time, in order to make recommendations for improving or changing international standards. In 1900, such a meeting was called and the International Bureau did make some changes. They agreed to adopt the *second*—a measure of time—as one of the basic standards.

Later, in that same year, Professor Giorgi of Italy recommended that, in addition to the standards of the meter, the kilogram and the second, a measure for electricity, the ampere, be included. (We will discuss the second and the *ampere* more thoroughly in a later chapter.)

Over the next 50 years no changes of importance were made. In 1954, the Tenth General Conference added two more units of measurement—one for measuring temperature, and another, the *candela*, for measuring luminous intensity or the brightness of light. A candela gets its name from one of our oldest forms of light, the candle flame. One of the early methods of measuring light was to say it was equal to one candle, or three candles. Of course, the candela is a much more scientific measurement. It is the heat given off by a very small (one square centimeter) black body heated to the temperature of the melting point of platinum. A black body is an object that *absorbs* all light instead of reflecting it. The absorbed light gives off heat, One candela is slightly less than one candle-power, a unit that is also used to measure light.

One of the most important general conferences of the twentieth century was held in 1960. This conference established the International Metric System or the *Systeme International d'Unites*. It had taken nearly 200 years, but the dream of the French scientists of the 1790's finally came true. The world had accepted the metric units as an international system. The international system, the Systeme International d'Unites, is known by engineers and technical people as *SI*.

SI lists and clearly defines six base units for length, weight, volume, temperature, electric power, force, pressure and other technical data which are derived from the six base units.

Another important change made by the Eleventh General Conference was the adoption of a unique, new method for measuring the length of a meter. The SI meter was not marked on a platinum bar. It was measured with

The entrance to the International Bureau of Weights and Measures in France.

light wave lengths! Scientists had discovered that a meter was equal to 1,650,763.73 wave lengths of the orange-red light given off by *Krypton 86*. Krypton is a rare gas that was not discovered until 1898. (The name Krypton came from a Greek word meaning "hidden," and was selected because the rare gas was hidden, or undiscovered, for so many years.)

Krypton has a very stable atomic structure, which means that it will not link or bond with other elements. Chemists say that its electrons will not "hold hands" with other electrons. Also, it is not affected by heat or cold.

The light waves of Krypton are very, very tiny and they do not change in size. So, the length of a meter based on these light waves is very accurate and can be tested or checked in any well-equipped physics laboratory. Even though the SI meter is actually based on the minute light wave lengths of Krypton 86, the traditional platinum-iridium bar is still kept at the International Bureau of Weights and Measures in France.

Although the SI units and wave length meter seem very accurate, scientists and researchers are constantly reviewing the international standards. General conferences will, no doubt, continue to meet in Paris to keep the international system up-to-date.

11. The Meter and the U.S. Yard

FOR MANY YEARS, the United States has attended many of the international conferences that developed the metric system even though it was not a metric nation. Yet, many people would say that in some respects the United States *was* actually a metric nation—even in its very early years.

On the wharves of many United States ports, cotton, wheat, corn and lumber were sold for years by the pound, bushel and foot. They were sold to metric countries. At the same time, products from metric countries were shipped to American ports. In order to avoid confusion, even before the Civil War, some United States industries were using a dual system of measurement (using both the customary inch-pound units, and the metric units).

Between the years 1854 and 1870, interest in metric measurement increased rapidly in the United States. In 1854, the American Geography and Statistical Society urged Congress to appoint a scientific commission to consider a uniform system of measurement based on a decimal system. This was to be the first of many such requests offered regularly by various U.S. groups during the next 120 years. The request was not acted upon.

Later, in 1863, even though the economy of the United States was shattered by the Civil War, the U.S. government did send representatives to two important international congresses. One, the International Statistical Congress, held in Berlin declared that

> . . . uniformity in weights and measures was of the highest importance, particularly for international commerce.

Binoculars and telescopes use metric units to measure their lenses.
This pair of binoculars has 50 mm lenses.

The second, a postal congress, held in Paris in May of this same year adopted the metric system for international postal service.

Trade and industry had been growing in the United States and so had interest in international standards for measurement. The use of the metric system by some groups —chemists, clockmakers, U.S. astronomers—was becoming quite common. So common, in fact, that in 1866 Congress passed a bill stating that it was:

> . . . lawful throughout the United States of America to employ the weights and measures of the metric system in all contracts, dealings or court proceedings.

Six years later, in 1872, the United States, as we saw in an earlier chapter, sent delegates to the Metric Convention in Paris, and was one of the 17 nations to sign the Treaty of the Meter in 1875. In 1876, a Metric Bureau was organized in the United States with headquarters in Boston, Massachusetts. Although the United States was not a metric nation, the metric system certainly was important to the U.S. Government and its people.

One reason why the metric system was important to the U.S. and was so frequently used was that the United States still had not established exact standards for the inch and the pound. Oddly enough, when Congress finally did join the International Bureau of Weights and Measures, it accepted the metric standards for its customary units. It adopted the international prototype meter and kilogram.

What did this mean? Most of the people in the United States used yardsticks and twelve-inch rulers to measure short lengths. When a family traveled from New York to California to visit Yosemite or San Francisco, they measured the distance in miles. Scales in stores used to weigh vegetables, fruit or meat were in ounces and pounds. Why did Congress think the United States needed a standard meter and standard kilogram? Why not simply develop a standard yard and pound?

Remember how the yard began? King Henry I said that a yard was the distance from the thumb on his outstretched arm to the tip of his nose. Who measured the distance? How could it be checked for accuracy? And what about the pound? Was it accurate? Great Britain, which had helped establish the first standards for the yard and the pound, had revised them during the early 1800's. But they were not *absolute* standards. An absolute standard does not change, and it can be checked and compared for accuracy at any time.

The metric system was clearly a more accurate system of measurement, and for this reason the U.S. was growing more and more interested in adopting it. Another reason was that by 1889, the metric standards were already adopted by 34 countries, including a neighbor country, Mexico, and several countries in South America.

So, in 1889, the United States joined the International Bureau. And delegates were sent to the International Conference of 1889 in Paris to receive prototype meter bars and kilograms. These bars and weights were carefully packaged and sealed and brought back to Washington, D.C. On January 2, 1890, President Benjamin Harrison broke the seals on the prototype meter and kilogram and they were deposited in a fireproof room of the U.S. Treasury Department's Office of Weights and Measures. The Treasury Department had supervised United States weights and measures since June 14, 1836, and it was the logical government department to keep the prototypes.

Three years after the prototype meter and kilogram were placed in the Office of Weights and Measures, the Secretary of the Treasury declared, ". . . from this date [1893] the meter and kilogram will be fundamental standards of length and weight for the United States." So, although the United States yard is considered to be 36 inches long, its *official* length is actually 0.9144 meters.

Eight years after the meter and kilogram became official standards for length and weight, a new government bureau was organized to be responsible for all U.S. weights and measures. In 1901, Congress established the U.S. National Bureau of Standards. At this time, the prototype meter and kilogram were moved from the Office of Weights and Measures to the National Bureau of Standards building. Since 1960, Krypton wave length standards established by SI have been used as an official standard for the meter, but the National Bureau of Standards still keeps a prototype meter bar and kilogram weight.

So, we see that although you and I use customary measuring *units*, the *standards* for the units have been the same as those of the metric system for many years.

12. Putting Metric Measurements to Work

THUS FAR YOU HAVE seen how the basic units of the metric system became basic units of the Systeme International d'Unites (SI), and the standards for measurement in the United States.

To understand any system of measurement, you must put the units to work. That's just what we are going to do. We are going to measure (mentally) length, weight and volume in metric units instead of in yards, pounds and quarts.

The easiest unit of metric measure to understand is the meter. The meter is used to measure length, width and height. Walk across a room. How wide is it? How long? How high is the ceiling? The answer to these questions would give us a measurement of length, or as it is often called, *linear measure.*

Linear measure follows a line: it has length. It may be very short, such as the width of a stick of chewing gum. Or, it may be very long—as long as the length (or distance) from New York to San Francisco, or even the distance from the earth to the moon.

How do you measure length, or linear measure, in meters? The first step is to learn the basic everyday metric units of linear measure. These are:

- *meter (m)* The meter is the basic unit of the metric system; it is slightly longer than the customary yard. It is abbreviated by using the letter **m**.
- *decimeter (dm)* The decimeter is one-tenth (1/10) of a meter, 10 decimeters = 1 meter. It is abbreviated by using the letters **dm**.

- *centimeter (cm)* The centimeter is one-hundredth (1/100) of a meter, 100 centimeters = 1 meter. It is abbreviated by using the letters **cm**.
- *millimeter (mm)* The millimeter is one-thousandth (1/1000) of a meter, 1000 millimeters = 1 meter. It is abbreviated by using the letters **mm**.

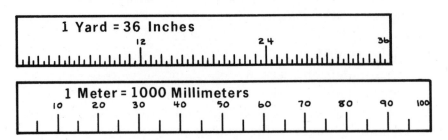

A meter is longer than a yard. One yard = 36 inches. One meter = 39.37 inches.

The decimeter is a basic part of a meter, but it is seldom used. As you will see later in this chapter, most metric lengths are described only in meters, centimeters, and millimeters.

Now that you know the names of the units, let's measure with them. But remember, this is going to be mental. It will not be exact; we will be estimating.

Look around you. Use items or people you see every day. For example, how tall are you? Your first impulse will be to answer in feet and inches, because feet and inches are familiar units of measurement to you. Don't think in familiar units. Think in metric terms.

What is the basic unit of the metric system? That should be familiar to you by now. It is the meter, itself. Are you shorter than a meter? Taller? Remember, a meter is slightly longer than a yard. A yard is three feet long. You must be taller than a yard, so you are more than a meter high.

Are you two meters high? Probably not. Most doorways are about two meters high. Do you know anyone two

TWO
YARDS
TALL

TWO
METERS
TALL

Here you can see the difference betwen a basketball
player two *yards* tall and one two *meters* tall.

meters tall? He or she would probably make a fine basketball player!

There are many other ways to think in metric units
without actually measuring with a meter stick or metric
ruler. Take a close look at the chairs in your kitchen or at
school. Most straight-back, wooden kitchen or desk chairs
are about one meter high. Compare the height of these
chairs with other objects around you. Do you see other
chairs, tables or desks that are one meter high or one meter
wide? How high is the sofa? How long? Most sofas are
about one meter high and two meters long. You see, it isn't
really so difficult to *think* in meters.

Look outside. Do you see anything that is two meters in
length or width? How about a bicycle? Take a good look at
a bicycle. think of the wooden desk chair. The bicycle is
about the same height as the chair, so the bicycle is ap-

proximately one meter high. It is about one and one-half meters long.

Look at a car. Cars are about as wide as a bicycle is long —one and one-half meters. Can you guess, or estimate, the length of a car in meters? Most cars are twice as long as they are wide, so the car is three to four meters long.

Many parts of a car and a bicycle are much smaller than a meter. They are measured in centimeters and millimeters.

What is a centimeter? A centimeter is 1/100 of a meter. It is about as wide as the tip of your middle finger. The distance across the palm of your hand, including your thumb, is about 10 centimeters. How wide is a book? How long is a pencil? Each is about twice as wide or long as the width of your hand. A book is about 20 centimeters wide, and a pencil is about 20 centimeters long.

Centimeters can be used to measure small objects, such as the thickness of a book, the height of a drinking glass or the width of a shoestring. But, some shoestrings are not very wide. Some are not even as wide as your finger or as wide as a centimeter.

Objects that are smaller than a centimeter are measured in millimeters. Ten millimeters equal one centimeter. Just think! Your finger is 10 millimeters wide! A millimeter is quite small. In fact, one millimeter is only about as wide as the lead in a sharpened No. 2 pencil.

Millimeters and centimeters are probably not new to you. Most rulers we use have millimeter and centimeter markings as well as inch markings. If you look at a ruler, you can quickly see that an inch is approximately equal to two and one-half centimeters or 25 millimeters.

Now that you know the approximate size of the basic units, let's see how these units are written to show measurement. Remember the bicycle? Its approximate length was one and one-half meters. If the bicycle were one and one-half yards, its length could be written as 1½ yards, or as one yard plus 18 inches. But the metric system uses neither fractions nor inches. Units of length are written in decimals. The length of the bicycle would be 1.50m, which means that it is one meter and 50 centimeters long. (100 centimeters = one meter, so 50 centimeters = one-half meter.)

The smaller parts of the bicycle are also written in decimals. Is the seat wider than your hand? Yes, it is probably about twice as wide as your hand. If your hand is approximately 10 centimeters wide, the seat is about 20 centimeters wide. This is written as *20cm* or *.20m.* (1 cm = 1/100 of a meter, so 20cm = 20/100 or .20 of a meter.)

Metric decimals are easier to understand if we remember that the number (or numbers) to the left of the decimal point indicate meters, the number (or numbers) to the right of the decimal point indicates centimeters. When you see a metric measure of 2.75, you must read it as two meters plus 75 centimeters.

Metric decimals are even easier to understand if you compare them to dollars and cents—which are also written in decimals.

If you have one dollar and 35 cents, you write it as $1.35. If a desk is one meter and thirty-five centimeters wide, you write it as 1.35m. If you earn two dollars and twenty cents, you have $2.20. And two meters and twenty centimeters is written as 2.20m.

1 dollar	$1 or $1.00
1 meter	1m or 1.00m
2, 3, 4, dollars	$2.00, $3.00, etc.
2, 3, 4, meters	2m or 2.00m, 3m or 3.00m, etc.
1 cent (100c = $1.00)	$0.01
1 centimeter (100cm = 1m)	.01m
2, 3, 4, cents	$0.02, $0.03, etc.
2, 3, 4, centimeters	0.02m, 0.03m, etc.

What happens if you have less than ten centimeters. Say you have six centimeters; how is that written? Six centimeters is written .06cm. Remember, the first two places after the decimal point are reserved for centimeters. If there are less than ten centimeters, the first number after the decimal point is a zero.

But, what about the millimeter? How is it written as a decimal? Remember, a millimeter measures lengths and widths that are less than a centimeter, and they are written in thousandths. For example, the width of a single link of chain on a bicycle is five to eight millimeters wide. This is written *5mm* to *8mm*, or as *0.005m* to *0.008m*. (One millimeter or 1mm = 1/1000 of a meter, so 5mm = 5/1000 of a meter, or 0.005m.)

Thus far, we have learned about the meter and two smaller units, the centimeter and millimeter. These are the measurements most frequently used to measure length. Now, let us turn to measurements that are larger than a meter.

Practice in Converting from Customary to Metric

AS WE LEARN ABOUT metric units, we will learn to measure length and distance with metric rulers and a meter stick. But, many customary measurements we use are very accurate. We do not have to re-measure all of them. We can convert customary units to metric units by multiplying. Let's look at some examples.

A room is 9 feet wide and 12 feet long. We want to know the metric dimensions. One foot equals approximately 30 centimeters, so if we multiply feet by 30 we can convert feet to centimeters.°

The room is 9 feet wide and 9 x 30 = 270, so 9 feet is approximately 270 centimeters or 2.70 meters.

° A more complete table of conversions for length, weight and volume is included in the appendix of this book.

The length of the room is 12 feet and 12 x 30 = 360, so 12 feet is approximately the same as 360 centimeters or 3.60 meters.

Our 9 by 12 feet room is approximately 2.70 by 3.60 meters.

You know how to change feet. Let's work with yards. An athlete is going to run the 100 yard dash in a track meet. How far will he run in meters?

1 yard = approximately 0.9 meters. We can convert yards to meters if we multiply by 0.9.

Since 100 x 0.9 = 90, the athlete sprinting 100 yards will cover about 90 meters.

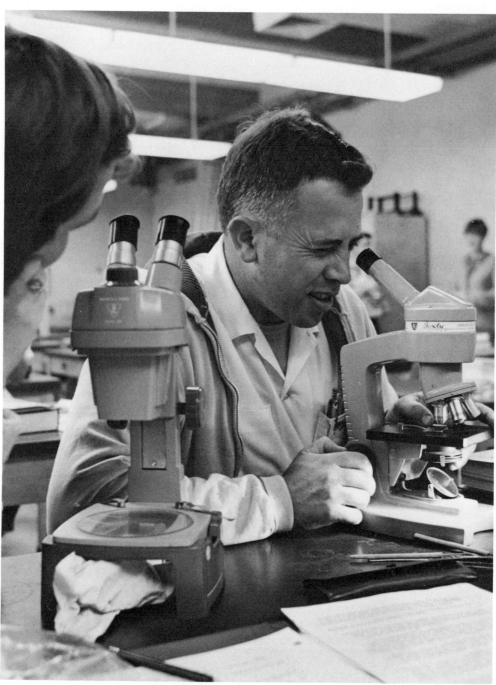

Microscopes such as these help scientists study items smaller than a micron.

13. Smaller and Larger Units of Measurement

SMALLER THAN A MILLIMETER! A millimeter is only about as wide as the point of a sharpened lead pencil, or the diameter of the wire of a small paper clip. Anything smaller than a millimeter, then, must be very, very tiny. Objects this small are measured by a very short unit of length called a *micrometer* or *micron*.

The prefix, *micro*, means small or minute. *Meter* means measure. So, a micrometer is a very small unit of measure. In fact, a micron is so small that it cannot be seen without a microscope. Scientists study bacteria, viruses and blood cells through a microscope because most of these items are as small or smaller than a micron, and cannot be seen by the naked eye.

Can you imagine making something as small as a micron? It is possible. The engineers of Western Electric have manufactured transistors for use in telephones that occupy less space than the cross section of a human hair! Parts of these transistors are only two to four microns thick.

A micrometer is one-thousandth (1/1000) of a millimeter. Think about that very carefully. One-thousandth of a millimeter! It takes 1,000 micrometers to make a millimeter. That means there are 1,000 micrometers in the tip of a pencil.

Just for fun, figure out the number of micrometers in a meter. Remember, there are 1,000 *milli*meters in a meter, and each millimeter equals 1,000 micrometers, or microns. How do you find the number of microns in a meter? Multiply the number of microns (1,000) by the number of millimeters (1,000). And the answer is:

1,000 microns per millimeter x 1,000 millimeters = 1,000,000 microns. There are one million microns in a meter!

A micron is so small, it is very difficult to imagine anything that size. But, there are items that are *even* smaller.

A *millimicrometer* (milli-micro-meter) is one-thousandth of a micrometer. This very small unit can be used to measure very, very tiny microscopic particles such as the length of a light wave. A millimicrometer is called a *nanometer*. It is one-billionth of a meter. (One billion nanometers equals one meter.)

One-trillionth of a meter is called a *micromicrometer* (micro-micro-meter), or a *picometer*. One trillion pico-meters equal one meter! What can possibly be this small?

An atom for one thing. An atom is so small that *250 million* atoms occupy the space of 25 millimeters (one inch). The average diameter of an atom is less than a micron, and the electrons inside an atom are as small as a picometer. Since nanometers and picometers are so extremely small, only very precise scientific equipment can measure their lengths.

In order to remember what we have said thus far in this chapter, let us list metric units smaller than a millimeter:

micron	**(one-millionth of a meter) one million microns equal one meter**
nanometer	**(one-billionth of a meter) one billion nanometers equal one meter**
picometer	**(one-trillionth of a meter) one trillion picometers equal one meter**

We can all agree that such small measurements are seldom used by the average person. After all, unless we are scientists, we will never need to measure anything we cannot see.

Now, let us turn our attention to metric units that are used almost everyday. Instead of being measurements of very small units, these measure large distances.

Go up, up, up and think in terms of great lengths and great distances. Think big! Think of lengths that are longer than a car or a house. Look across the fields and down the highways. These are lengths and distances that are longer than a meter.

Speed limits in metric countries are marked in kilometers instead of miles. A speed of 70 kilometers per hour is about the same as 44 miles per hour.

The most common unit in the metric system for lengths that are longer than a meter is the *kilometer* (kilo-meter). The prefix *kilo* means one thousand. A kilometer is 1,000 times longer than a meter. (1,000 meters equal one kilometer.)

A kilometer is used to measure distances from city to city, and even across continents from ocean to ocean. A tourist traveling along a highway in France, Sweden or Switzerland will see the highway distance signs marked in kilometers instead of miles. The kilometer is used in these countries, as well as in many others, to measure distance just as we use the mile in the United States. A kilometer, or *km* as it is abbreviated, is a little longer than a half-mile. It is 5/8 or .625 of a mile.

Will 95 kilometers be longer or shorter than 95 miles? Which will be the longer distance, 122 miles or 122 kilometers? Think . . . If one kilometer is shorter than one mile, then 95 kilometers will be shorter than 95 miles. And 122 miles will be a longer distance than 122 kilometers.

The kilometer is the common metric unit for distance, but there are terms for even greater distances, such as the *megameter* (one mega-meter = one million meters), *gigameter* (one giga-meter = one billion meters), and *terameter* (one tera-meter = one trillion meters). The megameter, gigameter, and terameter are all much, much longer than a kilometer.

Metric units larger than a kilometer are then as follows:

> **kilometer = one thousand meters**
> **megameter = one billion meters**
> **gigameter = one billion meters**
> **terameter = one trillion meters**

These units are rarely used except for measuring distances in space. And even for distances in space, astronomers and scientists usually use other measurements —such as the light year.

A light year is the distance that light travels in one year. And since light travels very, very fast—186,000 miles per second—a light year is a long, long distance.

In one year, light travels 9,464 terameters or 9,464,000,000,000 (nine trillion, 464 billion) kilometers! Or 5,878,000,000,000 (five trillion, 578 billion) miles!

Just look at the numbers. It is difficult to work with numbers of this size. No wonder astronomers and scientists prefer to work with light years instead of miles, meters or terameters.

You have read about the meter, the backbone of the metric system. You can estimate your height in meters and you know that a kilometer measures distance along a highway. You also know that, using picometers, scientists can measure things they cannot see with the naked eye.

Now, let's turn from the measurement of length to the measurement of weight.

This road sign in Switzerland shows that it is 68 kilometers (about 43 miles) to Chur.

Practice in Converting from Customary to Metric

MANY MILES OF INTERSTATE and country lanes are accurately measured and marked all across the United States. We can find the metric distances for these miles without actually measuring them.

One mile equals approximately 1.6 kilometers. If we know the number of miles, we can find the number of kilometers by mutiplying by 1.6.

On a sunny afternoon you take a bike hike with some friends. You ride five miles out to your favorite fishing spot. How far will you ride in kilometers? Multiply the miles you ride by 1.6. 5 x 1.6 = 8. You will ride 8 kilometers on your bike hike.

Your Grandmother lives 20 miles away. Can you compute the distance to your Grandmother's home in kilometers? Multiply miles (20) by 1.6 as we did in the problem above and you travel 32 kilometers one way, each time you visit Grandmother. 20 x 1.6 = 32.

Now, let's go a long, long way. Let's catch a plane in New York and fly across the United States to San Francisco. The plane travels approximately 3,000 miles. How far is 3,000 miles if we measure them in kilometers?

3,000 x 1.6 = 4,800

It is approximately 4,800 kilometers across the United States.

14. Grams and Kilograms

THE METER and all of its larger and smaller units measure length. We have discussed the meaning of length and how it is written or described in metric units. We have also learned that a gram is the weight of a cube filled with water, and that is one centimeter long, one centimeter wide and one centimeter high. But, before we can really understand the meaning of a gram and its use, we should know more about the word *weight*.

Weight is the "heaviness" of an object. One of the earliest methods used to measure heaviness was the balance (which we discussed in Chapter Three). The balance measured weight by comparing one object to another. If you, yourself, compare the weights of two different objects, you will better understand how a balance or scale works.

Pick up a tennis ball, hold it in your left hand. In your right hand, hold a round rock that is approximately the same size as the tennis ball. You can feel the difference between the ball and the stone. One is light; the other is heavy. This heaviness or lightness is what a balance or scale measures.

You cannot measure the exact weights of the stone and the ball, but you know that one is heavier than the other. The stone feels heavier because it takes more energy to hold it than the tennis ball. This heaviness is caused by *gravity*.

The word gravity comes from the Latin word *gravis*, meaning heavy. Gravity is the force that holds stones, trees, houses and even people down, and keeps them from floating off the surface of the earth. The pull of gravity on an object is commonly called *weight*.

In the U.S. customary system, weight is measured in ounces and pounds. An ounce measures small amounts of weight. Sixteen ounces equal one pound.

The gram and the kilogram of the metric system are also used to measure weight just as the ounce and pound are used in the U.S. customary system. Grams measure small quantities. One thousand grams equal one *kilogram*.

There are, however, two major differences between the customary and metric units. The weight of a pound is less than a kilogram, but the weight of an ounce is heavier than a gram. In fact, an ounce is *28 times heavier than a gram*. Twenty-eight grams are approximately the same weight as one ounce. So you can see a gram is very small and light.

Even though a gram is small and light, many items that we use daily weigh a gram or less. A paper clip weighs about one gram. A grain of golden "popped" popcorn weighs less than a gram. One whole peanut, out of the shell, weighs about one gram. So, it would take one thousand shelled peanuts to equal one kilogram! (A kilogram, you will remember, is equal to 1,000 grams.)

A gram may be much smaller than an ounce, but a kilogram is heavier in weight than a pound. One kilogram = 2.2 pounds. Four quarter-pound sticks of butter or oleomargarine equals one pound, but it takes eight and one-half sticks of butter or oleomargarine to equal a kilogram.

The gram (abbreviated *g*) and kilogram (abbreviated *kg*) are the two most common units of metric weight. The larger and smaller units of metric weight were created and named using the same method as was used to name the larger and smaller units of the meter. The gram was divided by 10, 100 and 1,000 to determine the smaller units. And it was multiplied by 10, 100 and 1,000 to determine the larger units.

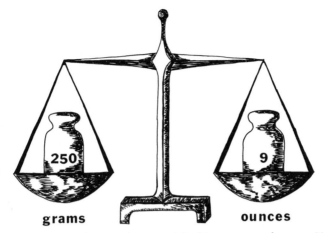

Smaller items such as candy are weighed in ounces and grams. Nine ounces of candy will weigh approximately 250 grams.

Smaller than a gram:

1 centigram = 1/100 of a gram (100 centigrams = 1 gram)

1 milligram = 1/1000 of a gram (1,000 milligrams = 1 gram)

Larger than a gram:

1 kilogram = 1,000 grams

1 megagram = 1,000,000 grams (1,000 kilograms) = 1 metric ton

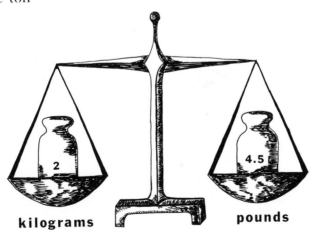

Kilograms and pounds weigh items such as fruits and vegetables. A 2 kilogram ham weights about 4.5 pounds.

These are the metric units of weight. How do you use them? Most of the work in using grams or kilograms is easy. It is like weighing an object or objects in ounces and pounds. The scale does the work. We only have to read the amount.

For example, let's think of weighing a sack of candy on an *avoirdupois scale* (the kind of scale we are used to using in the United States). Watch the arrow move along the numbers of the scale. The numbers of this scale tell us the weight of the candy in ounces and pounds. Let's say the candy weighs 1 pound and 8 ounces.

Now let's weigh the same candy on a *metric scale*. The numbers on the metric scale show us the weight of the candy in grams and kilograms. When we read the weight of the candy on this scale we see it weighs 674 grams.

You will probably be greatly surprised the first time you weigh anything, including yourself, on a metric scale—

This metric scale measures weight and computes the total price of the item when it is given the price per kilogram. This scale was designed in Britain.

unless you remember that a kilogram is more than twice as large as a pound. But, since we have a tendency to think of the kilogram and the pound as being the same, the first time we use a metric scale, the weight we read on the scales will seem too little.

For example, a 165-pound man will weigh 75 kilograms. A 105-pound girl or boy will weigh 46 kilograms. How much do you weigh in pounds? 80-90 pounds? Then you weigh only 36-41 kilograms! Your weight did not change from scale to scale. Only the unit of measurement changed. The weight of *any* object in kilograms is less than the weight of the same object given in pounds.

Make a short grocery list of some foods you use often in your home and then pretend you are shopping in a "metric" store. Put on your list: bulk sausage or ground beef, sugar, flour, preserves, cinnamon and milk.

How many pounds of sausage would you like to buy? About two to three pounds? Then, you must ask the meat-cutter for 1 to 1.25 (one and one-fourth) kilograms of meat. What size bag of sugar and flour does your mother buy? Ten pounds? Then, you will probably buy five kilograms of each. Do you like strawberry preserves? A one-pound jar will weigh 454 grams.

The cinnamon will be much lighter than the meat, flour, or preserves. Cinnamon, pepper, and other spices are finely ground and weigh very little. They will be measured with grams or milligrams (mg.). A one-ounce can of cinnamon will be marked 28 grams.

You have everything except the milk. You want to buy two quarts of milk. How many kilograms will equal two quarts? Wait! Something is wrong. Quarts? Kilograms? Milk isn't sold by the kilogram. Milk is a liquid and liquids have another unit of measurement in the metric system. Before we can finish our shopping trip we must learn more about measuring liquids.

Practice in Converting from Customary to Metric

SAY YOU WOULD like to know how much you weigh in kilograms, but you don't have a metric scale. In the last two chapters we learned how to convert feet to meters and miles to kilometers by multiplying. We can compute metric weight the same way if we know the weight in pounds. When we know the number of pounds, we can find the number of kilograms if we multiply by .45.

How much do you weigh? Let's say you weigh 90 pounds. 90 x .45 = 40.50. If you weigh 90 pounds, you weigh approximately 40.50 kilograms.

Your brother weighs 102 pounds. How much does he weigh in kilograms. 102 x .45 = 45.90. Your brother weighs approximately 45.90 kilograms.

A weight lifter is working out in the gym. He lifts 100 pounds above his head. How many kilograms is he lifting? 100 x .45 = 45. He is lifting approximately 45 kilograms.

15. Liters for Liquids

LIQUIDS, MILK, WATER, juices and other semi-liquid products, are measured by *volume*. And, as we learned in an earlier chapter, volume is the amount of space a liquid occupies. Sound confusing? Then think of it this way: volume is the·amount of liquid a given container will hold.

Volume, of course, varies according to the size of the container. For example, a large coffee mug will hold more (has more volume) than a dainty tea cup. And the volume of a large gasoline tank of an automobile is more than the volume of the gasoline tank of a motorcycle.

For years you have measured volume, large and small, in ounces and quarts. However, if you have ever helped with science experiments in school, you know you can also measure volume in *milliliters* and *liters* instead of ounces and quarts.

Just what are liters and milliliters? Let's look first at the liter, the larger of these two basic metric measurements for volume. The liter (abbreviated *l*) is very similar in size to the quart with which you are familiar, but it is slightly larger. One liter = 1.06 quarts. It is probably easier to remember that a quart is a little *less* than a liter of milk or water. A quart of water will fill four standard eight ounce cups. A liter will fill four and one quarter cups.

Many, many items (grape juice, milk, cooking oil) are sold by the quart in the United States. But supermarkets and corner grocery stores in metric countries sell these items by the liter. It isn't just food products that are measured by the liter. Many other products such as oil for

1 Quart

1 Liter

A liter is slightly larger in volume than a quart. 1 liter = 1.06 quarts.

automobiles are sold by the liter and when motorists in Japan, Austria and Sweden say, "Fill 'er up," the gasoline that goes into the tank of their cars is measured by liters. Almost any item that can be sold by the quart in the United States is sold by the liter in metric countries. But, what about liquids, like liquid shampoos, nail polish, or small bottles of decorative enamel paints for model airplanes and cars? How are liquids that are less than a liter measured?

The milliliter (1,000 milliliters = one liter) measures amounts of liquids smaller than a liter. A milliliter (abbreviated *ml*) is a very small quantity—so small that it takes five milliliters of liquid to fill one teaspoon! The use of this small unit of volume corresponds to the use of the U.S. customary liquid ounce. But, the volume or space occupied by a milliliter is smaller than the volume of one liquid ounce.

If someone said to you on a hot day, "Shall I pour you 30 milliliters of cola *or* one ounce?" you would probably choose 30 milliliters because you are accustomed to thinking that an ounce is quite small; but you also know that eight ounces equal a cup. So 30 milliliters sounds like more than one ounce. They are, however, approximately the same. Thirty milliliters equal one liquid ounce. Would you

5 Milliliters = 1 Teaspoon

15 Milliliters = 1 Tablespoon

Milliliters measure very small quantities of liquid. It takes five milliliters of liquid to fill one teaspoon. Fifteen milliliters = one tablespoon.

like to have 250 milliliters of cola of your favorite drink? Sounds like a lot, doesn't it, and yet 250 milliliters is approximately the same as an eight ounce can or bottle of cola which is only about one cup.

The use of the milliliter is not new in the United States. For years, nearly all medicines have been measured in milliliters in both metric and non-metric countries. Pharmacists measure liquid ingredients for prescriptions in milliliters and if you look along the shelves of the drug store or pharmacy you will find many items marked with milliliters (ml). A bottle of nose drops is often marked 30 ml and some liquid vitamins are 250ml.

There are other units for measuring volume besides the liter and milliliter. But, the larger units, such as a *kiloliter*, are seldom used except by industries that handle large quantities of liquid products, such as the petroleum industry. And the smaller units are seldom used except by engineers and technical people.

Smaller than one liter:
    deciliter = one-tenth (1/10) of a liter
    centiliter = one-hundredth (1/100) of a liter
    milliliter = one-thousandth (1/1000) of a liter

Larger than one liter:
  dekaliter = 10 liters
  hectoliter = 100 liters
  kiloliter = 1,000 liters

Recognize the prefixes? Notice how "centi," "hecto," "kilo," and "milli" are used with all the basic units of the metric system. Can you relate the prefixes to the other units . . . the meter and the gram? Notice that "centi" and "kilo" always have the same meaning. Centi is smaller than the basic unit and means the unit measure is one-hundredth of the basic unit. Kilo means 1,000 and that the new unit is 1,000 times larger than the basic unit.

Meters, liters and grams are the most frequently used metric or SI units. Let's find out about some other basic measurements. They are considered "basic" but they are a little more complex than measuring the length of a room, the weight of a can of peaches, or the contents of a glass of milk.

Practice in Converting from Customary to Metric

MANY LIQUIDS WE BUY or use are pre-measured for us. Others like gasoline for our cars, motorcycles and lawn mowers are not measured. We usually buy gasoline by the gallon. But, when we change to the metric system, we will buy gasoline by the liter.

The gasoline tank of the average American car holds 20 gallons. How many liters can be put in this same car?

We can convert gallons to liters if we multiply the number of gallons by 3.8. The 20 gallon tank will hold approximately 76 liters (20 x 3.8 = 76.0).

Let's look at another example. Your friend rides a Honda 175cc motorcycle. Its gasoline tank holds two gallons. How many liters does it hold?

2 x 3.8 = 7.6. The motorcycle tank will hold 7.6 liters of gasoline.

Some liquid quantities we measure are very small. Think of the recipes we use when we cook. Recipes often ask for a tablespoon of water, a teaspoon of vanilla, or a cup of milk or water. How much is a cup of milk measured in milliliters?

A standard measuring cup holds 8 ounces and we can convert ounces to milliliters if we multiply ounces by 30. A cup—8 ounces—of milk or water will be approximately 240 milliliters. (8 x 30 = 240).

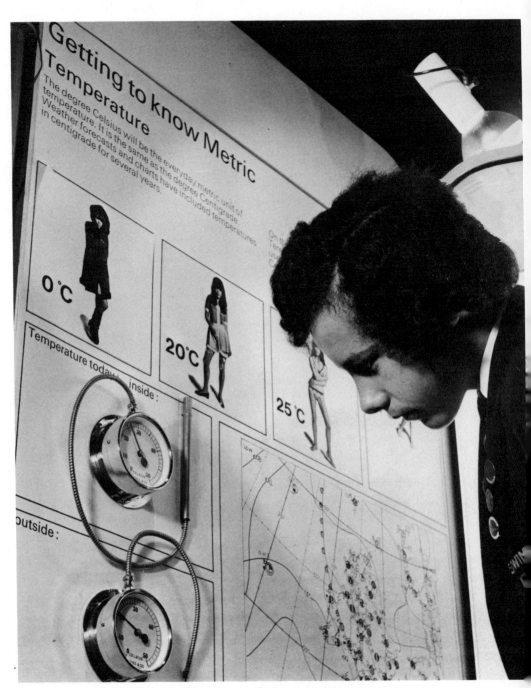

A young British boy studies metric temperature units.

16. Seconds, Degrees and Amperes as Units of Measurement

WHEN THE FRENCH first planned their new metric system, their most important goal was to establish units for length, weight and volume. These units are the backbone of any measuring systm.

In the nineteenth century, when these units were first established, they were the types of basic measurement used everyday—and they were practically the only types needed. Today, however, with television, air conditioning, swift automobiles and adventuring into outer space, there are may other kinds of measurement that are required, and are increasingly important.

Today, we even measure *time* much more accurately than ever before. Men have measured time for many years. Some of the very early "timekeepers"—sundials and simple hourglasses—date back to the days of the Babylonians, but these early timekeepers measured mostly the hours of the day. In the twentieth century, so many factories, airlines, railroads and other daily events depend on very accurate schedules that time is measured in *hours, minutes* and *seconds*. It is measured by all sizes and shapes of clocks and watches.

The hands and numbers of a clock or watch tell us how long to practice our violin, do our homework or even how long we must bake a cake or cook a pot roast. The entire mechanism of a clock is a measuring instrument. It is measuring time. The basic units of measurement for time—

seconds, minutes and hours—are not all decimal, but they *are* a part of the international metric system.

Another important unit of measurement that is important to our everyday lives is *temperature*. Are you warm? Hot? Cold? Quite comfortable, perhaps. Warmth and coldness are controlled by heat. We use many different types of heat. We heat our homes, schools and factories on cold days. We cook food on stoves with heat. Our bodies contain heat and, if we get too warm, we perspire and are uncomfortable. If we get too cold, we shiver. When we are sick, our bodies are too warm and we say we have a fever. All these forms of heat—heat for homes, factories, cooking and even the heat in our bodies—are measured by temperature.

The basic unit for the measurement of temperature is a *degree* (the symbol for degree is °) and degrees are

This thermometer has Fahrenheit units on the left and Celsius units on the right.

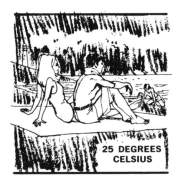 

The National Bureau of Standards in Washington has printed illustrations such as these to help Americans think metric.

measured by a *thermometer*. The word thermometer is
made up of *thermo*, which means unit of heat, and *meter*,
which means to measure.

There are two basic methods of measuring or, as we
sometimes say, recording temperature. One is called
Fahrenheit; the other *Celsius*. Both are named after the
men who invented the scales or thermometers that measure
degrees of heat. Countries which use the metric system,
usually measure temperature in degrees Celsius.

A Fahrenheit thermometer is the one we use most often
in the United States. When the mercury on the Fahrenheit
thermometer shows that the temperature outside is 32° or
lower, you know that ice will freeze and windshields will be
frosty. When the temperature on a Fahrenheit thermometer reads 85° or more, it is a fine day for sailing or
swimming.

In 1742, a Swedish astronomer, Anders Celsius, experimented with another temperature scale that was easier
to use. Celsius' thermometer was called *centigrade* for
many years. Centigrade means "one hundred steps" and
the basic scale of the Celsius thermometer runs from 0° to
100° rather than from 32° to 212° as on the Fahrenheit
thermometer that we use in the United States.

The freezing point on a Fahrenheit thermometer is 32°

but when a thin layer of ice freezes, the mercury on a Celsius thermometer will read 0° or less. On a hot sunny day in July, a Fahrenheit thermometer will read 90° to 95° while a Celsius thermometer will read 32° to 34°. Nearly every country in the world uses the Celsius scale to record temperature and scientists in America have always preferred to use Celsius just as they have preferred to work with meters, liters and grams.

The chart below shows how the two basic types of thermometers will read when the temperature is the same.

Freezing point of water	0° Celsius	32° Fahrenheit
Normal body temperature	36.9° Celsius	98.6° Fahrenheit
Boiling point of water	100° Celsius	212° Fahrenheit

The lowest temperature on this chart is 0° and the highest 212°, but degrees of temperature can go much lower than zero and much higher than 212°. Just think how hot molten steel must be. Molten steel has temperatures that go above 3000° Fahrenheit! Many industries— petroleum, glass, potteries, plastics—depend on very high temperatures (400° F, 650° F, 3200° F) for making their products.

Temperature can also be very, very cold. We think it is cold when we go out on a windy winter day and the temperature is zero. Zero does seem quite cold, but we know temperatures can go below zero on both Fahrenheit and Celsius scales. Thermometers in North Dakota and some of the provinces of Canada often record temperatures of -40° F and lower during the winter months. If you go outside in such weather, it is bitterly cold. But, is this really cold? How cold can cold be? Nobody has ever made anything cold enough to measure the coldest cold or the lowest limits of coldness. Physicists working in laboratories have come very, very close—within a fraction of a degree—and they call this point or degree of coldness *absolute zero*. This is the point at which absolutely no heat will register on any known scale used for measuring heat.

On a Celsius scale, absolute zero would be -273°; on a Fahrenheit scale -459°. Physicists who work with extremely low temperatures do not usually work with Celsius or Fahrenheit. They measure heat, or the lack of it, with the Kelvin scale. Absolute zero is the lowest temperature on the Kelvin scale. What is the highest temperature of the Kelvin scale? It is very difficult to imagine absolute zero or no heat at all and it is virtually impossible to imagine the upper limits of this scale. Perhaps the closest we can come would be to think of the heat of the sun. On a Celsius scale the heat of the sun is estimated to be 40,000,000°!

Most of the heat we measure everyday comes directly from the sun, but heat is also created by electricity and other sources of energy. We use electricity for many things in our homes—light bulbs, radios, televisions, blenders. It is an important source of energy that is measured. You are familiar with some measuring devices for electricity, such as electric meters, and we frequently see the symbols for the units of measurement (ampere, watt, volt) on light bulbs and other electrical appliances. The method of measurement of electricity and other types of power is part of the international system, but it is rather complex and we will not discuss it in this book.

The units of measurement for time, temperature and electricity are the last of the six base units of the international system.

17. An Island in a Metric Ocean

IT WAS NOT UNTIL the 1950's that the international units that we have been discussing—the meter, the gram and the liter—became an increasingly important subject of discussion to the people of the United States. This has happened because more and more frequently, in recent years, many people have been recommending that the United States become a metric nation like other nations. Why has this pressure for change been building up? Let's examine just a few of the more important reasons.

Probably the most important reason is that we are living in a space age. In 1957, a Russian rocket soared upward into space, and the first man-made satellite, Sputnik, began to orbit the earth. Launching the first successful satellite was like opening a "Pandora's Box" filled with all kinds of scientific surprises. Research in all fields of sciences—physics, chemistry, medicine and electronics—more than doubled shortly after 1957, and many exciting inventions and discoveries were made.

In 1969, *men*, not just satellites, were orbiting the earth. And then, men began to walk on the moon! This achievement required the use of very exact measurements for every tiny part that went into the making of a rocket. Electronic equipment, computers, and thousands of other products had to be produced to exact measurement and had to be trouble-free. Scientists and engineers had long used metric units for their research in space projects so it was logical that metric units were being used in the U.S. space program. Astronauts even measured their first trips on the surface of the moon in kilometers. When the astronauts sent back their television reports they used metric units. Many Americans received their first exposure to the metric system in this way.

It wasn't just rockets that were measured in centimeters and other metric units. Metric units were soon being used for all kinds of equipment that required precise measurement—tiny transistor radios, fast modern trains and complex lifesaving medical equipment. Thousands of workers in many industries were becoming more and more familiar with the metric system. Scientists, engineers, and many technical people began to encourage the adoption of the metric system by the United States.

Technical people were not the only ones interested in the adoption of the metric units. As the space age progressed, a big change was occurring in United States industry. Great manufacturing companies like General Electric, John Deere and Ford Motor Company were not just shipping products overseas, they were building plants overseas. For example, in 1973, the Caterpillar Company of Peoria, Illinois, which makes bulldozers, roadgraders and other earth movers, said, "The sun never sets on Caterpillar." They meant that they had plants and offices in every continent of the world.

Another company, General Electric, had been active in South Africa since 1894 and in the 1970's G.E. was doing business in 37 countries. These companies—Caterpillar, General Electric, John Deere—and many others were no longer one-country industries. They became multinational, manufacturing products in many parts of the world.

Executives, engineers and mechanics of these companies worked side by side with foreign engineers who used the meter and kilogram as the unit of measurement. Many of their drawings were "dual-dimensional." They were scaled

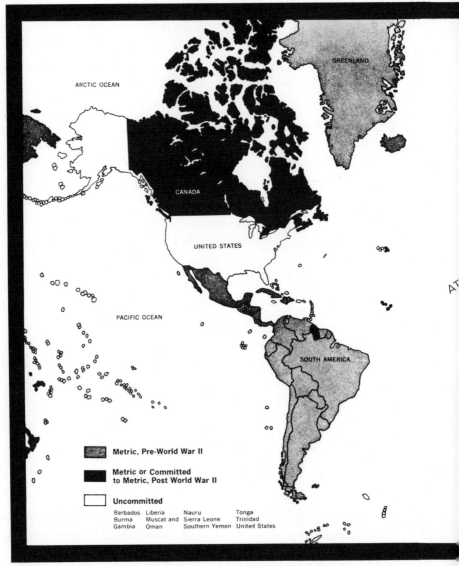

ARCTIC OCEAN

GREENLAND

CANADA

UNITED STATES

PACIFIC OCEAN

SOUTH AMERICA

AT

Metric, Pre-World War II

Metric or Committed
to Metric, Post World War II

Uncommitted

Barbados	Liberia	Nauru	Tonga
Burma	Muscat and	Sierra Leone	Trinidad
Gambia	Oman	Southern Yemen	United States

in both inches and millimeters. Engineers and U.S. companies who used only the inch-pound system were definitely in the minority.

By 1960, 90% of the countries in the world were metric countries, and talk of the United States "going metric" became stronger and stronger. Representatives of many industries in addition to many political leaders felt that the time had come for the United States to use metric units as official measuring.

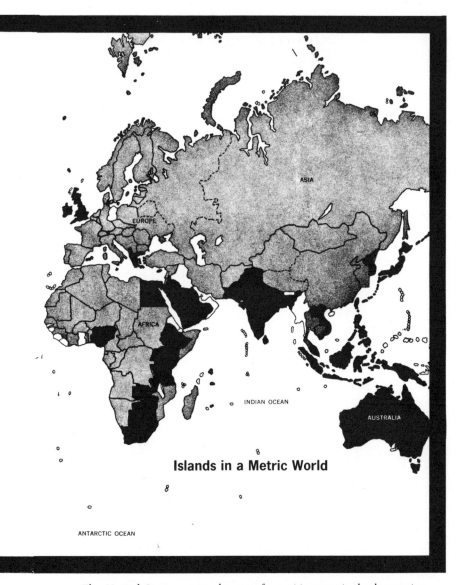

Islands in a Metric World

The United States, as can be seen from this map, is the last major country in the world to accept the metric system. Other countries which have not accepted it include Burma and Liberia.

Some disagreed, however. It is not a real problem, they argued. Canada, our neighbor to the north uses many of our products—and they are a non-metric nation. Great Britain is also non-metric. They agreed that we could survive as a non-metric country.

Then, in 1965, the Parliament of Great Britain voted to become a metric nation. And Canada was making plans to change. Suddenly, the United States became an island in a metric world. It stood almost alone!

Many Americans, including scientists, leaders of industry and congressmen, began to think more seriously about the need to become a metric nation. As Great Britain began the monumental task of metrication—of changing from imperial to metric units—the U.S. kept a close eye on the progress of the changeover. They would be able to learn how to go about it when the time came for the U.S. to make the change.

18. Great Britain Abandons Use of Imperial Units

GREAT BRITAIN, like the United States, spent much time, during the twentieth century, thinking about going metric. England's leaders had known, for many years, that it was important for them to change over from the yard and the inch to metric units. But, getting this done in real life was a difficult job.

Pretend that you are a carpenter. Think of all the changes you would have to make if you measured with meters instead of yards. Look in your tool box. Do your scales and tapes have centimeters as well as inches? Not all. This means you will have to replace many tools, and this will involve quite an expense to you. If certain tools have not been manufactured yet, it will involve even more problems and expense.

As you begin a day's work, you have plans and drawings to follow. Are they metric? Architects and draftsmen would have to convert all measurements and drawings to metric units. Again, there would be a great deal of time wasted and money spent. And then, there is the lumber—rafters, supports, trimwood . . . if you call the lumber yard, do they have your supplies measured in metric units? If not, they would have to remark all of the pieces of lumber that you need.

So you can see from this one small example how changing over a system of measurement from one method to another involves many groups of people—government

A large M on a cube over the British flag is Britain's symbol for the changeover to metric units.

agencies, industries, retailers, farmers, schools, construction workers. You can also see how troublesome and expensive the process can be.

In 1968, the British Minister of Technology reported that metrication of industry can be efficient and economical only if *all* groups work together. That is a big order!

Even after the decision was made in England to convert, it took two additional years of planning before the changeover could begin. During this time, a Metrication Board was formed to help make the change easier for factories, stores and their employees. Schools began to teach metric measurement on all levels. Colleges began familiarizing teachers with metric units and helped them create effective ways of teaching. From the very beginning, educators not only taught students to substitute the metric system for the imperial system, but also to *think* metric. In fact, that is where the emphasis of the entire British program was placed: on *thinking* metric.

The cargo liner Tabaristan, here docked in England, was one of the first ships built in Great Britain which has bow markings in meters as well as in feet.

Posters of all sizes and shapes were put in public buildings, stores and factories.

WEIGH IN KILOGRAMS!
KEEP A COOL HEAD—36.9° C
THINK METRIC

These posters were used to help train the average family to think in metric terms. At work and at home, people began to use the new measuring system.

Unfortunately, Great Britain had a two-fold problem as she adopted the metric units. Although many countries of Europe had a decimal system for currency, Britain did not. A French franc was equal to *100* centimes, a Dutch gilder contained *100* cents, and a German mark consisted of 100 pfenning. But, until 1971, the British pound consisted of 20 shillings each containing 12 pence. Britishers had much less experience with decimal computation than did people in other countries.

As Britain made the changeover to decimal measuring units, she also made the change to decimal coinage. The new pound was now equal to *100 new pence.*

As the public was learning to think metric, it was also learning to think decimal in both currency and measurement. And there were problems. Just imagine going to the store and having to think . . . a kilogram is equal to 100 grams, so a 250 gram package is the same as 2.50kg. After buying several items you would feel a little bewildered. Then it is time to pay. You hand the clerk a five pound note. For change you get a new pound note and some new coins. Oh dear, you ask yourself. Is the change correct? Let's see . . . the new pound is worth 100 pence and this seven sided coin is worth fifty pence, so . . . .

As you can see, learning two decimal systems at once can be confusing.

British women volunteers help erect metric signs along a footpath near Winchester, England.

Despite some of these problems, in February, 1971, the country officially became a decimal currency country, and was halfway through a ten-year metrication plan.

By 1971, industries such as the construction industry, the electric power industry, railroads, telephone companies, and major airlines were using metric measurements in most of their operations. Some of the more complex industries, such as the automotive industry, were progressing much more slowly. But, Great Britain was fortunate, because the very industries which were affected the most by the metric changeover had been the leaders in requesting metrication. And this made the job a lot easier than if the giant industries opposed the change.

Metrication in England is not yet complete, and even when it is, imperial units of measurement will continue to be used for many years to come. Habits of the past are not easily changed. As one British gentlemen has said, "We may be officially adopting the metric system, but I shall continue to walk a *mile* to my favorite pub, not 1.6 *kilometers!*"

As Great Britain is gradually becoming a metric nation, the United States continues as the only major country in the world still using exclusively inches, feet and pounds.

19. U.S. Officials Recommend Adoption of Metric Study Group

AFTER GREAT BRITAIN began metrication in 1965, United States senators and representatives not only watched the progress of the British conversion, but started to consider using the meter and gram system here. Actually, they realized that the metric system was already here. Many professionals—scientists, doctors and pharmacists— had been using the metric system for quite a long time. Another factor that made the U.S. leaders begin to think. seriously about, adopting the metric system was that our neighbor to the north, Canada, would before long surely follow in the footsteps of England and other nations of the British Commonwealth.

Canada was already preparing to make the change but was waiting for the United States. Many Canadian officials thought it would be easier if the two countries made the changeover together. But how long would Canada wait?

The time had come for something to be done. The question was, should it be left to time—with the new system taking root here in an unorganized way—or should a plan be adopted so the metric system would be adopted in a gradual, but organized way?

Ever since 1854, many bills and recommendations favoring the adoption of the metric system had been sent to Congress, but they had not been passed. Finally, in August, 1968, a bill proposing a thorough study of the metric system was adopted and became Public Law 90-472.

Public Law 90-472 had been drafted by Congressman George P. Miller (California), Senator Claiborne Pell (Rhode Island), and Senator Robert P. Griffin (Michigan). It authorized the Secretary of Commerce

> . . . to conduct a program of investigation, research, and survey to determine the impact of increasing worldwide use of the metric system on the United States.

The act also authorized the Secretary of Commerce to investigate all advantages and disadvantages of the international system of weights and measures which were being used all over the world. After three years, a full report of his findings and recommendations was to be sent to Congress.

Very soon after the bill was passed, a metric research organization was set up at the National Bureau of Standards in Washington, D.C. This metric study group worked with many other government departments and agencies.

For three years, members of this study group interviewed business executives, engineers and scientists. They talked to men assembling stereos on factory lines. They visited stores that sold materials by the yard, and potatoes and flour by the pound.

Could these factories and their employees work with meters? Could the stores sell material in meters and weigh potatoes in kilograms? Members of the study group asked hundreds of questions. What machines had to be changed or replaced? What did the machines cost?

Dozens of detailed reports from industries, colleges, and unions were sent to the Metric Study Office in Washington. Companies already using some metrics were visited many times. Researchers studied Great Britain's program. They could learn much from Britain, Japan, and other countries that had changed over to the metric system.

It had taken Japan nearly 40 years to get her people to use a meter instead of a *shaku* (Japan's former unit of

[WORKING DRAFT NO. 1]

OCTOBER 4, 1973

93D CONGRESS
1ST SESSION

S. 100

IN THE SENATE OF THE UNITED STATES

JANUARY 4, 1973

Mr. PELL (for himself and Mr. INOUYE) introduced the following bill; which was read twice and referred to the Committee on Commerce

[Strike out all after the enacting clause and insert the part printed in italic]

A BILL

To provide a national program in order to make the international metric system the predominant but not exclusive system of measurement in the United States and to provide for converting to the general use of such system within ten years.

1   *Be it enacted by the Senate and House of Representa-*

2 *tives of the United States of America in Congress assembled,*

3   ~~SHORT   TITLE~~

4   ~~SECTION 1. This Act may be cited as the "Metric Con-~~

5 ~~version Act of 1973".~~

6   ~~FINDINGS~~

7   ~~SEC. 2. The Congress finds that—~~

8   ~~(1) the United States is the only industrially~~

This is a working draft of a bill to make the metric system official in the United States introduced by Senators Pell and Inouye.

measurement for length), and a gram instead of a *kan* (measurement for weight). During the 40 years, Japan had many problems. At times, the changeover was not only very confusing, but very expensive as well.

Britain organized its changeover better. It had set its goals better and had less problems. In 1970, in their ten-year metrication program, meters had taken the place of yards in many industries. It experienced less confusion than Japan that devoted 40 years to making the change.

It seemed as though Great Britain's program was a good example for the U.S. to follow. And this opinion was reflected in the recommendations made by Secretary of Commerce Maurice Stans, in August, 1971. He made the following recommendations to Congress:

1. That the United States change to the international metric system deliberately and carefully.

2. That this be done through a coordinated national program.

3. That early priority be given to educating every American school child, and the public at large to think in metric terms.

4. That Congress establish 1981 as a target date for the changeover.

In August, 1972, after careful study of the recommendations and the detailed reports of the metric study, the Senate passed a bill introduced by Senator Claiborne Pell. The bill proposed a changeover to the metric system. It included many of the recommendations that had been made by the Secretary of Commerce. Although the senate passed the bill, the House did not act on the bill and it "died."

In 1973, bills for metric conversion were again introduced in both Houses of Congress. The House bill was introduced by Representative Olen E. Teague (Texas) and the Senate bill once again by Senator Pell and Senator Inouye (Hawaii). Neither of the bills were brought before

Congress for a vote by January, 1974, but Senator Inouye reported that Congress would hopefully act soon on this legislation. The basic points of the bills were:

1. Setting a changeover period of 10 years as the time goal.

2. The creation of a national Metric Conversion Board.

3. The establishment of a national information program.

The U.S. Metric Study had provided many facts and vital information about the use of the international system of units in the United States. The bills, when passed, will make the changeover official. But even this will be just a beginning. The actual changeover will depend on the special efforts of thousands of people plus those of every citizen.

20. Getting Used to Something New

THE AVERAGE AMERICAN paid little attention to the U.S. Metric Study or to the bills proposed by Congress. Large food companies, manufacturers and automotive industries, however, have been very interested in both. In fact, some had participated in the study and were in favor of the bills. Companies like Ford, John Deere, and Caterpillar had already started the changeover. Some of their design engineers have been working with metric scales for several years and new products were already being designed with metric units.

In the early 1970's, Ford Motor Company designed the Pinto and put it into production. Many cars used in the United States—Volkswagen, Opel, Mazda—were "metric" cars, but the Pinto was the first American-made car with a metric engine design. "The Pinto is just the beginning," the Ford Motor Company reported. "We will soon have an all-metric car."

In 1972, Caterpillar Tractor Company reported to a Senate committee on commerce that they were in favor of legislation to bring about the adoption of the metric system, and that they were already making new designs in metric measure in anticipation of the adoption of the system on a national basis.

During 1972, other large companies (General Motors, for example) also began to make plans to use more metric measurements. Some companies organized special "metric training sessions" for their employees. Some even started schools. Research engineers and draftsmen began to discuss

This is the engine for a Ford Pinto. The Pinto engine was the first metric engine built in the United States.

office procedures. They were interested in discovering the best way to begin using the international units.

Each major company will have individual changeover procedures, but each will follow a similar plan to conversion. The use of metric units in most industries usually begins at the design board. At first, new machines and products will be drawn with millimeter and centimeter dimensions. Some will replace old designs and prints. Others will be drawn for totally new machines, trucks or automobiles. As the new machines and equipment go into production, they will be built with nuts and bolts already in stock (so as to use up the old stock of parts) as well as some new metric parts. Gradually, all of the individual designs and parts will be metric.

This is not as complex as it sounds. New tractors, trucks and other machines are being designed and redesigned every year. In a period of eight to ten years, many components manufactured by almost every industry fail to meet their own modern standards for new equipment. As these old parts are changed for newer and better designed parts, they will be changed to metric measurements.

Adopting the metric system will take at least 10 or more years for some, industries. Others, such as those that produce chemicals, petroleum and textiles will make the change more quickly. Many of these companies will only need to replace or adjust measuring devices. Gas stations will adjust pumps to measure liters instead of gallons. Fabric stores will sell bolts of material by the meter instead of the yard.

Some businesses, such as the railroads and public utilities that supply electric power and gas, will change very little. Many will not change at all, because they already use the system. Pharmacists have measured many liquid and dry medicines in milliliters and milligrams for years. Cameras and camera equipment have, for a long time now, been

Engineers in Ford's Body Engineering Office in Dearborn, Michigan.
Metric conversion begins at the drawing board.

following metric unit measurements. The same is true for Americans who slalom down the snow slopes of Vermont and Colorado on skis. Skis have always been measured in centimeters and, of course, all of the sparkplugs in our automobiles have always been measured in millimeters.

When the United States adopts the international system of units, how will the changeover affect you? At first you will see very little difference. For several years, your mother will continue to measure material by the yard and use her regular measuring cups. The units and measuring devices with which you are familiar will not change immediately.

"Going metric" for you will be much easier than "going metric" for industry and manufacturing companies, because, as John L. Feirer, the first director of the nation's Center for Metric Education said, "Most people will need to learn only three measurements—those for length, weight and volume."

Much of the early changeover will undoubtedly begin in the schools, just as it did in Britain. Thousands of U.S. schools are already teaching metric measurements in science and math classes. They are following the British idea of teaching the actual use of metric units, instead of how to convert from one system to the other. Jeffrey V. Odom of the Metric Information Office in Washington, D.C., pointed out that "it is best if both students and teachers learn to use metric units by measuring familiar things in metric units only." Then, he added, "I warn against a general attempt to teach metric equivalents and conversion factors from customary to metric and vice versa."

Emphasis now, and in the future, will be on the idea of learning by doing. Even very young elementary students will measure desks, rooms and art projects in meters and centimeters. They will do problems in class using the

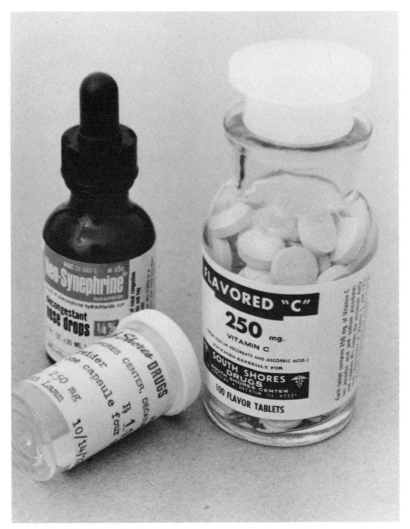

Medicines—both liquid and dry—have been measured in milligrams and milliliters for years.

decimal metric system.

As you begin to learn and use the metric units, you will still weigh yourself in pounds. But, as the metric conversion continues, you will weigh yourself on scales marked in kilograms. Milk will be sold by the liter. The weatherman will give his reports using degrees in centigrade (Celsius), instead of fahrenheit as he does now. Before long, you will realize that he has not made a mistake when he gives a temperature of 35° for a sunny day in July. And while all this is happening, owners of stores will be getting new scales so they can weigh meat and bananas in grams and kilograms.

While these changes are happening slowly, you will be driving in your car one day, and will notice that the speed limit signs have been changed. Instead of saying 30 m.p.h. (miles per hour), the speed limit will be given as 48 km (48 kilometers per hour).

Many common measures will change only as tradition changes. And only time will tell us which ones will cling the longest. No doubt apples and peaches will continue to be sold in bushel baskets and football fields will continue to be measured in yards for many years.

The new liters and meters and grams may be a bit confusing for awhile,. But, as metric units become more and more familiar, and are used in more and more stores, schools and homes, you will find them easy to understand. You will begin to "think" metric. You will not think your thermometer is broken if in the summer months the temperature is 30°, and you will not think your scale is broken if it says you weigh 50 or 60.

Appendix

Table of Conversions

As much as possible we should "think metric," but sometimes you will want to convert customary units to metric or metric to customary. This is how you do it:

	When You Know:	You Can Find:	If You Multiply By:
Length	inches	millimeters	25
	feet	centimeters	30
	yards	meters	0.9
	miles	kilometers	1.6
	millimeters	inches	0.04
	centimeters	inches	0.4
	meters	yards	1.1
	kilometers	miles	0.6
Weight	ounces	grams	28
	pounds	kilograms	0.45
	short tons	megagrams (metric tons)	0.9
	grams	ounces	0.035
	kilograms	pounds	2.2
	megagrams (metric tons)	short tons	1.1
Liquid Volume	ounces	milliliters	30
	pints	liters	0.47
	quarts	liters	0.95
	gallons	liters	3.8
	milliliters	ounces	0.034
	liters	pints	2.1
	liters	quarts	1.06
	liters	gallons	0.26

Converting temperatures from degrees Fahrenheit to degrees Celsius and from degrees Celsius to degrees Fahrenheit is a bit more complicated. To go from Fahrenheit to Celsius, subtract 32° from the Fahrenheit temperature and then multiply the result by 5/9. The result is temperature in degrees Celsius. To go from Celsius to Fahrenheit, multiply the temperature in degree Celsius by 9/5 and add 32°. It is necessary to add and subtract 32° because the freezing point of water is 0° in Celsius and 32° in Fahrenheit. The following formulas can be used:

Degrees Fahrenheit = 9/5 degrees Celsius + 32°
Degrees Celsius = 5/9 x (degrees Fahrenheit - 32°)

Using the Conversion Table

LET'S TAKE AN IMAGINARY TRIP into a metric country and see how the table of conversion can help us as we travel. We often think of European countries as being metric but, did you realize that Mexico, our neighboring country directly to the south, is also a metric country. Let's take our imaginary trip south of California to the beautiful Baja country of Mexico.

Soon after we cross the border we will begin to see speed limit signs marked in kilometers. One of the first signs along the road tells us the speed limit is 85 kilometers per hour. What will be the correct speed on a car speedometer marked in miles per hour?

Look at the conversion chart. We did some problems like this in Chapter 13, Remember? We know the number of kilometers. Since we want to find miles, we multiply by 0.6. $85 \times 0.6 = 51$. So we can travel safely at 50 miles per hour.

On the trip we pass through Ensenada and soon see road signs telling us the distance to the next village. A road sign reads: Ojos Negros 15 KM. How far away is this village in miles? $15 \times 0.6 = 9.0$. Ojos Negros is approximately 9 miles away.

We travel on down the winding road and stop to buy gasoline. We want to buy 5 gallons. The pump measures gasoline in liters. How many liters do we ask the station attendant to put in the tank?

Look at the table of conversion for liquid volume. When we know gallons—in this case, 5 gallons—we multiply by 3.8 to find liters. $5 \times 3.8 = 19.0$. Instead of asking for 5 gallons, we ask for 19 liters.

You have seen how the tables work for visitors going to a metric country, now let's see how a visitor from a metric country can use them when he is traveling in the United

States. A family from Sweden is traveling along Interstate 55 south of Memphis, Tennessee. The speed limit sign tells them they must not go over 55 MPH. What is the speed limit in kilometers? We change miles to kilometers by multiplying by 1.6. 55 x 1.6 = 88. The speed limit on the interstate is approximately 88 kilometers per hour.

As the Swedish family travels along, they see a road sign that tells them Memphis is 25 miles away. How many kilometers is it to Memphis? 25 x 1.6 = 40. The family must travel approximately 40 more kilometers before they reach Memphis.

When they arrive in Memphis they stop to visit some friends and also buy some groceries for a picnic. They buy marshmallows, potato chips and two pounds of hot dogs. How much will the hot dogs weigh in kilograms? As you can see on the table, we can convert pounds to kilograms if we multiply by .45. 2 x .45 = .90. Two pounds of hot dogs is less than 1 kilogram. They weigh approximately .9 kilograms.

They also need some milk. At home in Sweden they usually buy 2 liters of milk when they go to the store. How many quarts will they buy in Memphis? We have had some problems in which we worked with gallons and liters. But how do we change liters to quarts? If you know liters and want to find quarts you multiply by 1.06. 2 x 1.06 = 2.12. The Swedish family will probably buy two quarts or 1 half-gallon.

If you are lucky enough to take a trip abroad, it would be a good idea for you to keep in mind some of the conversion constants needed to convert from the metric system to the customary system.

Glossary

ampere—a unit of measurement for electric current.

avoirdupois—a measuring system for weight using ounces and pounds; 16 ounces = 1 pound.

body measurement—the use of parts of the body to measure length.

carat—the weight for measuring diamonds and other precious stones standardized in 1913. A carat weighs 200 milligrams, or one-fifth of a gram.

cube or cubic—having dimensions of height, length, and width which are exactly equal.

cubit—one of the oldest body measurements; believed to be the distance of a man's forearm from his elbow to the end of his index finger. Cubits were used to build some of the ancient Egyptian pyramids. The word is used very often in the Bible.

decimal system—a number system based on the number 10 and its multiples. "Deci" means ten. A typical decimal system is the U.S. currency system.

electric current—a stream of moving electrons.

gram—a metric unit of measure for weight; equal to the weight of one cubic centimeter of water. A gram is very small, about the weight of a paper clip.

gravity—the pull or force that holds objects on the earth;

122

from the Latin word "gravis," meaning heavy.

Imperial System—a "family" of measuring units established by Great Britain. Includes the yard, gallon, and pound; similar to the U.S. customary system except that some of its units of measure do not have the same standards. For example, a royal gallon is greater than a U.S. gallon.

International Bureau of Weights and Measures—an international organization with headquarters near Sevres, France, established shortly after 1875. It does research and helps coordinate standards for international trade.

Krypton—a rare chemical element; a gas that belongs to the "noble gases" (neon, helium, argon) that are chemically inactive and do not link or bond with other elements. Because of its inactivity Krypton is used as a measuring standard.

libra—an ancient term for the Roman "pound."

light year—a unit of measurement for long distances in space; the distance light travels in one year; approximately 6,000,000,000,000 miles or 9,464,000,000,000 kilometers.

linear measurement—measurements or dimensions that follow a line, such as length, width and height.

liter—a unit of measure for volume; equal to the space occupied by a cube 1 decimeter x 1 decimeter x 1 decimeter. Slightly larger than 1 quart (about 1.06 quarts).

measurement system—a "family" of units and standards used together to describe measurements of length, weight and volume.

meridian—lines of longitude on a globe or map that circle the earth running north and south from pole to pole.

meter—the basic metric unit of measure for length; slightly longer than a yard (39.37").

metrication—Great Britain's name for her national changeover, or conversion, from the imperial to metric system, which began in 1965.

micron—a nickname or common term for a micrometer which is one-millionth of a meter.

microscopic—tiny, minute; not visible without the aid of magnifying equipment.

National Bureau of Standards—the official U.S. government agency of weights and measures established in 1901 as a part of the Department of Commerce to provide technical assistance to industry, government, and educational institutions and to help with the development, maintenance, and provide information about fundamental standards of physical measurement.

prototype—a first sample which becomes the model for other copies. International standards or prototypes of the meter and kilogram, made of a special alloy of platinum and iridium, are kept at the International Bureau of Weights and Measures. See *standards* for more information.

quadrant—one-fourth of a circle; one-fourth of a meridian, such as the distance of length of a meridian from the North

Pole to the equator.

SI—nickname or common term for systeme international d'unites.

standards—basic units or references for measurement, also called prototypes. Exact duplicates of the standard meter and kilogram are kept at the International Bureau of Weights and Measures. Exact duplicates of these standard measures have been sent to every government represented at the Bureau. In the United States, they are kept in the Bureau of Standards in Washington, D.C. They were first received by President Benjamin Harrison on January 2, 1890.

Systeme international d'unites—international system of units established in 1960 to coordinate world-wide use of metric standards. Commonly known as SI.

unciae—an ancient Roman term for an inch *and* for *an ounce*. meaning one-twelfth. Twelve divisions of a foot = one unciae (inch) and twelve unciae = one libra (pound).

U.S. customary system—a "family" of measuring units established by the United States which includes the inch, foot, yard, pound, pint, and quart.

watt—a unit of electric power. A watt measures the power needed to make a light bulb glow or a fan run.

weight—the heaviness of an object caused by the force or pull of gravity.

INDEX